Claire Merrills

Cambridge IGCSE® and O Level
Accounting
Revision Guide

CAMBRIDGE
UNIVERSITY PRESS

CAMBRIDGE
UNIVERSITY PRESS

University Printing House, Cambridge CB2 8BS, United Kingdom

One Liberty Plaza, 20th Floor, New York, NY 10006, USA

477 Williamstown Road, Port Melbourne, VIC 3207, Australia

314-231, 3rd Floor, Plot 3, Splendor Forum, Jasola District Centre, New Delhi - 110025, India

103 Penang Road, #05-06/07, Visioncrest Commercial, Singapore 238467

Cambridge University Press is part of the University of Cambridge.

It furthers the University's mission by disseminating knowledge in the pursuit of education, learning and research at the highest international levels of excellence.

www.cambridge.org
Information on this title: www.cambridge.org/9781108436991

© Cambridge University Press 2018

This publication is in copyright. Subject to statutory exception and to the provisions of relevant collective licensing agreements, no reproduction of any part may take place without the written permission of Cambridge University Press.

First published 2018

20 19 18 17 16 15 14 13 12 11 10 9 8 7 6 5

Printed in Great Britain by CPI Group (UK) Ltd, Croydon CR0 4YY

A catalogue record for this publication is available from the British Library

ISBN 978-1-108-43699-1 Paperback

Cambridge University Press has no responsibility for the persistence or accuracy of URLs for external or third-party internet websites referred to in this publication, and does not guarantee that any content on such websites is, or will remain, accurate or appropriate. Information regarding prices, travel timetables, and other factual information given in this work is correct at the time of first printing but Cambridge University Press does not guarantee the accuracy of such information thereafter.

....

NOTICE TO TEACHERS IN THE UK
It is illegal to reproduce any part of this work in material form (including photocopying and electronic storage) except under the following circumstances:
(i) where you are abiding by a licence granted to your school or institution by the Copyright Licensing Agency;
(ii) where no such licence exists, or where you wish to exceed the terms of a licence, and you have gained the written permission of Cambridge University Press;
(iii) where you are allowed to reproduce without permission under the provisions of Chapter 3 of the Copyright, Designs and Patents Act 1988, which covers, for example, the reproduction of short passages within certain types of educational anthology and reproduction for the purposes of setting examination questions.

All exam-style questions and sample answers in this title have been written by the author. In examinations, the way marks are awarded may be different.

®IGCSE is a registered trademark.

Contents

Introduction		iv
How to use this book		v
Section 1		**1**
1	Introduction to accounting	2
2	Double entry book-keeping – Part A	9
3	The trial balance	19
4	Double entry book-keeping – Part B	26
5	Petty cash books	35
Section 2		**43**
6	Business documents	44
7	Books of prime entry	51
Section 3		**59**
8	Financial statements – Part A	60
9	Financial statements – Part B	69
10	Accounting rules	76
11	Other payables and other receivables	83
12	Accounting for depreciation and disposal of non-current assets	91
13	Irrecoverable debts and provisions for doubtful debts	100
Section 4		**107**
14	Bank reconciliation statements	108
15	Journal entries and correction of errors	116
16	Control accounts	127
17	Incomplete records	135
18	Accounts of clubs and societies	143
19	Partnerships	154
20	Manufacturing accounts	162
21	Limited companies	171
22	Analysis and interpretation	178
Answers to examination-style questions		186
Answers to progress check questions		255
Index		261
Acknowledgements		266

Introduction

How to use this Revision Guide

This Revision Guide is designed to help you revise all the topics in your Cambridge IGCSE® and O Level Accounting course. Each chapter summarises a key accounting topic and is based on a section of the syllabus. Every chapter includes:

- learning summary setting out what you should understand by the end of the chapter
- definitions and explanations of key concepts
- sample questions accompanied by exemplar answers so that you can follow through the logic and approach. Accounting is a practical subject and it is by attempting questions, checking them and making a list of errors that you can learn and improve your accounting understanding and technique
- tips to remind you of a key point, advise you of a common error or offer guidance on how to approach a question
- a progress check – questions to check your understanding
- a revision checklist – a short summary of what you should know
- Examination-style questions – a variety of multiple choice questions, short answer questions and longer structured answers to complete. All of the answers are at the back of the Revision Guide so that you can instantly check your learning.

The difference between paper 1 and paper 2

Both papers are based on all syllabus content and there are no options for questions so all are compulsory. Paper 1 is worth 30% of the total examination and is 35 marks of multiple choice questions. Multiple choice questions consist of:

- a stem or introduction that states what is required
- four possible choices or responses – A, B, C, D.

A useful approach to accounting multiple choice questions is to decide your answer before looking at the options available, so you are not distracted by similar answers. Always make an attempt and never leave a multiple choice answer unanswered.

Paper 2 is a structured written paper of 100 marks which is worth 70% of the examination. You will be presented with a variety of tasks for example, carrying out calculations, completing a cash book, and preparing the financial statements for a sole trader, partnership, manufacturing organisation, limited company or clubs and societies.

Assessment objectives (AOs)

This is the technical term for the skills that will be tested in the examination. Accounting is a skills-based subject, as well as demonstrating knowledge and understanding, you need to be able to analyse and evaluate information.

Knowledge and **understanding** – you should be able to:

- demonstrate knowledge and understanding of facts, terms, principles, policies, procedure and techniques that are in the syllabus
- demonstrate understanding of knowledge through numeracy, literacy, presentation and interpretation and apply this knowledge and understanding in various accounting situations and problems.

Analysis – you should be able to:

- select data which is relevant to identified needs of business
- order, analyse and present information in an appropriate accounting form.

Evaluation – you should be able to:

- interpret and evaluate accounting information and draw reasoned conclusions.

How to revise

Revision should be an ongoing process throughout your course as your teachers will test you on topics at regular stages as you progress. The revision materials you build up on topics can then be used in preparation for your final examination.

1. **Know what you need to learn.** Ask your teacher and use your coursebook to ensure that you are familiar with all the content.
2. **Revise effectively.** It is better to revise in small chunks of time. Revising with friends can also help as you may have strengths in different areas and can support each other.
3. **Make your revision active.** This is easy to achieve in Accounting as it is not an essay-based subject. Flash cards, mnemonics and mind maps are good for learning definitions and advantages and disadvantages for topics. For the more complex areas, this Revision Guide provides examination style questions to help you prepare – but you should also practice past examination paper questions.
4. **Put the hours in.** You wouldn't expect to pass your driving test after one hour of practice. Research has proved the more hours you commit to revising, the better the outcome in terms of grades. But remember that the revision needs to be active and focus on the areas you are least familiar with or find the hardest.
5. **Practice past examination papers.** It is strongly advised that you practice past examination papers, using the knowledge contained within the Revision Guide to help.

Things to remember

1. Always have a calculator with you.
2. Show your workings for calculations.
3. Be precise with definitions.
4. If you are asked to make a judgement, use supporting evidence from your calculations to illustrate your points.

How to use this book

This Revision Guide complements the IGCSE and O Level Accounting coursebook and aims to help you consolidate your accounting knowledge and understanding and develop the skills of analysis and evaluation. It has been designed as a flexible resource to support you on your accounting skills journey and advance your knowledge and understanding of key topics. The questions are designed to provide further opportunities for you to check your ability to provide solutions to a variety of accounting problems and practise your accounting skills.

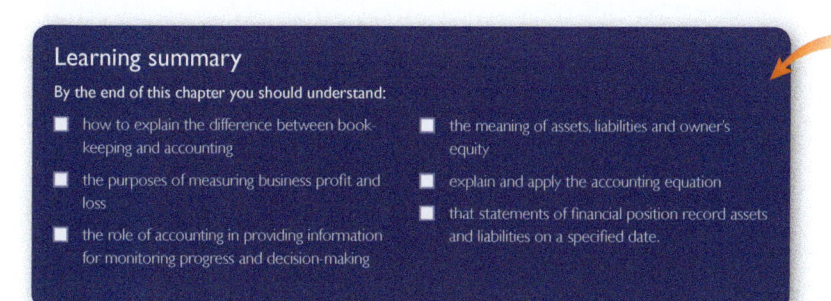

Learning summary

By the end of this chapter you should understand:

- how to explain the difference between book-keeping and accounting
- the purposes of measuring business profit and loss
- the role of accounting in providing information for monitoring progress and decision-making
- the meaning of assets, liabilities and owner's equity
- explain and apply the accounting equation
- that statements of financial position record assets and liabilities on a specified date.

Learning summary — Each chapter begins with the key accounting concepts that you will learn to help you navigate your way through the book and remind you what is important about each topic for your revision.

Tips — Tips provide additional content, reminders and useful information about key points.

TERMS

Accounting is the process of using the information collected by the book-keeper to calculate key measures such as a business's profit or loss and what the business owns (assets) and owes (liabilities).

Assets are items a business owns or amounts owed to them by others. They can be categorised as current assets (to be used within the business with the aim to make profit, i.e. cash or inventory) or non-current assets (large, expensive items such as machinery and premises which stay longer in a business but also help to generate profit).

Book-keeping is the recording of a business's financial transactions. These transactions are placed in the books of prime entry.

Liabilities are amounts owed by the business to others and they can also be current (within the financial year or next 12 months) or non-current (due for repayment after the end of the current financial year or over 12 months).

Loss is when total costs exceed total revenue.

Owner's equity or capital represents the amount of money or assets, such as machinery or vehicles, an owner introduces into the business. It is essentially what the business owes to the owner.

Profit is when total revenue exceeds total costs.

TIPS

Think of assets as being positive items you would be happy to have. Liabilities aren't necessarily bad, as often a business needs to borrow to expand, but on a personal level you would rather have lots of assets and few liabilities.

Owner's equity isn't necessarily just cash or bank amounts introduced by the owner. It could be equipment or a motor vehicle. This can increase throughout the business's life depending on what the owner's plans are and does not just happen at the start of the business.

Progress check

1. What is the difference between book-keeping and accounting?
2. State the accounting equation.
3. Define assets, liabilities and owner's equity.
4. What does a statement of financial position show?

Progress check — Questions provided to check your progress as your proceed through the book.

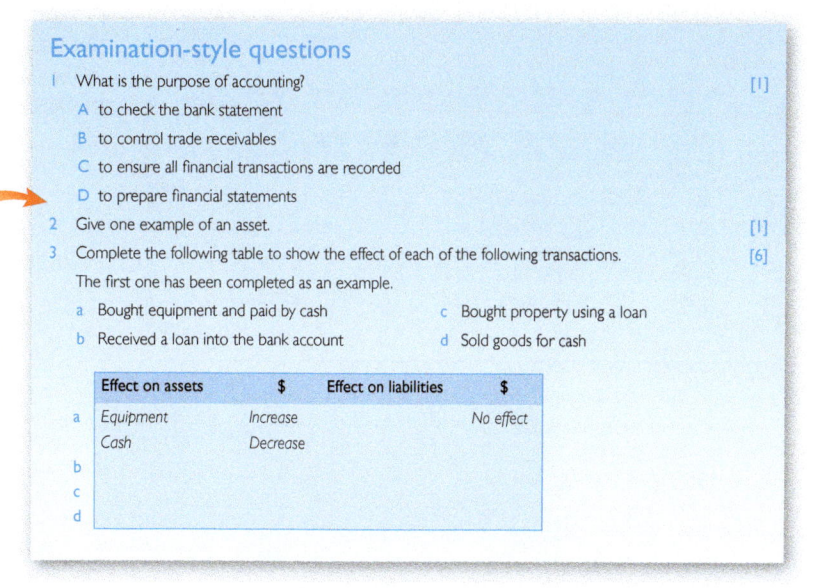

Terms — Definitions help you identify and understand important accounting terminology and concepts.

Examination-style questions

1. What is the purpose of accounting? [1]
   - A to check the bank statement
   - B to control trade receivables
   - C to ensure all financial transactions are recorded
   - D to prepare financial statements
2. Give one example of an asset. [1]
3. Complete the following table to show the effect of each of the following transactions. [6]
   The first one has been completed as an example.
   - a Bought equipment and paid by cash
   - b Received a loan into the bank account
   - c Bought property using a loan
   - d Sold goods for cash

	Effect on assets	$	Effect on liabilities	$
a	Equipment Cash	Increase Decrease	No effect	
b				
c				
d				

Examination-style questions — Examination-style questions will help you familiarise yourself with the style of questions seen in examination and assess your own understanding and skills to answer them.

Sample questions

1. Calculate the missing amounts:

Assets $	Owner's equity $	Liabilities $
150 000	100 000	
	84 000	35 000
48 000		22 500

Answer:

Assets $	Owner's equity $	Liabilities $
150 000	100 000	**50 000**
119 000	84 000	35 000
48 000	**25 500**	22 500

2. A business may employ both a book-keeper and an accountant. What is the role of the book-keeper?

A to make financial decisions about the business's future

B to prepare income statements at regular intervals

C to record all the financial transactions of the business

D to summarise the assets and liabilities of the business

Answer: The answer is C. The book-keeper could be involved in all sorts of aspects of a business and its finances. However, their primary role is to record all the financial transactions of the business. This information is then used by the accountant to produce financial statements.

3. State whether each item is an asset or liability by ticking next to each item the category in which it belongs:

	Asset	Liability
Motor vehicle		
Bank overdraft		
Trade payables		
Trade receivables		

Answer:

	Asset	Liability
Motor vehicle	✓	
Bank overdraft		✓
Trade payables		✓
Trade receivables	✓	

Sample questions — Sample questions and answers are designed to guide you through best practice when answering accounting questions.

Revision checklist

In this chapter you have learnt:

- the difference between book-keeping, recording financial transactions and accounting which uses the book-keeping records to prepare financial statements and to assist in decision-making
- the purpose of measuring business profit and loss is so that a business owner can makes plans according to the outcomes
- the role of accounting in providing information for monitoring progress and decision-making
- the meaning of assets, which represent items owned by or owing to the business; liabilities, which represent anything owed by the business; and owner's equity, which is also known as capital and is what the business owes to the owner
- the accounting equation which is Assets – Liabilities = Owner's equity or capital
- that statements of financial position record assets and liabilities on a specified date and also show the owner's equity.

Revision checklist — Checklists at the end of each chapter provide a useful summary of the learning points covered.

Introduction to accounting

1. D [1]
2. One from: property, motor vehicle, inventory, bank, cash or trade receivables. [1]
3.

	Effect on assets	$	Effect on liabilities	$	
a	Equipment	Increase		No effect	[1]
	Cash	Decrease			[1]
b	Bank	Increase	Loan	Increase	[1]
c	Property	Increase	Mortgage	Increase	[1]
d	Inventory	Decrease			[1]
	Cash	Increase			[1]

[6]

Answers — Answers to examination-style and progress check questions can be found at the back of the book, use these to check and reflect on your progress as you work through the Revision Guide.

Section 1

Chapter 1

Introduction to accounting

Learning summary

By the end of this chapter you should understand:

- ☐ how to explain the difference between book-keeping and accounting
- ☐ the purposes of measuring business profit and loss
- ☐ the role of accounting in providing information for monitoring progress and decision-making
- ☐ the meaning of assets, liabilities and owner's equity
- ☐ explain and apply the accounting equation
- ☐ that statements of financial position record assets and liabilities on a specified date.

TERMS

Accounting is the process of using the information collected by the book-keeper to calculate key measures such as a business's profit or loss and what the business owns (assets) and owes (liabilities).

Assets are items a business owns or amounts owed to them by others. They can be categorised as current assets (to be used within the business with the aim to make profit, i.e. cash or inventory) or non-current assets (large, expensive items such as machinery and premises which stay longer in a business but also help to generate profit).

Book-keeping is the recording of a business's financial transactions. These transactions are placed in the books of prime entry.

Liabilities are amounts owed by the business to others and they can also be current (within the financial year or next 12 months) or non-current (due for repayment after the end of the current financial year or over 12 months).

Loss is when total costs exceed total revenue.

Owner's equity or capital represents the amount of money or assets, such as machinery or vehicles, an owner introduces into the business. It is essentially what the business owes to the owner.

Profit is when total revenue exceeds total costs.

Differences between book-keeping and accounting

It is essential that every business keeps track of its transactions in order to accurately calculate profit or loss at the end of the financial year. However, perhaps more important for the business owner themselves, keeping track of transactions enables them to make accurate decisions which will allow their business to grow. One of the main objectives of a business is to maximise profit, but profit cannot be calculated unless we record every transaction coming into and out of the business. Book-keeping is the straightforward recording of the original transactions into the books of prime entry and then into ledger accounts. The books of prime entry will be explored in a later chapter but just think of them as a reminder of where money has been spent or earned or inventory has been purchased on credit, for example. Purchasing on credit is a popular way for businesses to carry out transactions as it involves the inventory being delivered to the customer but payment is not required for several weeks. By the time payment is required the goods will hopefully have been sold for a profit. It is calculating the profit or loss which is the responsibility of the accounting function.

Book-keeping does not prevent errors happening or ensure accuracy. If an error has been made in the initial recording of a financial transaction then it will be revealed by the original document and may not come to light unless a supplier or customer questions the amount involved.

The purposes of measuring business profit and loss

Using the information recorded by the book-keeper the accountant is then able to produce two key documents which help to contribute to a business's financial statements. The first of these is the income statement which has a misleading name as it not only records the income but also the expenses of the business. This then allows the accounting staff to calculate the profit, if income exceeds expenses, or loss, if expenses exceed income. The statement of financial position also contains the key profit or loss for the year which is calculated in the income statement. In addition, this statement shows the assets and liabilities of the business. This, put simply, is what the business owns and owes and how it has been funded through the owner's equity.

Information for monitoring progress and decision-making

On a more practical level, decisions such as whether to increase staff pay, whether to find a cheaper supplier and whether external loans are needed can be explored. How can important decisions be made within a business unless they know if they are able to generate a profit? A business will not last long if it purely focuses on its bank and cash balances.

The accounting year for a business is a 12 month period which is often determined by when the business started. An income statement shows income and expenses for a period of time, whereas a statement of financial position shows assets and liabilities at a particular time.

Assets, liabilities and owner's equity

When a business is started resources are needed in the form of money, inventory of goods, property and motor vehicles (depending on the type of business). These resources may be funded by the owner or by external borrowing, perhaps using a bank loan. The owner can introduce money or any other types of assets which they think appropriate, such as a delivery van. Whatever they decide to contribute to the business is known as the owner's equity or capital. The more owner's equity available, the less will need to be borrowed from other sources.

The assets are the items which the business owns or are owed to them. For example, if the business sells goods on credit to a customer (receive the goods and pay later), this customer is now a trade receivable and owes money for the goods they have received.

Liabilities are amounts which the business owes. The business may have a bank overdraft, a bank loan or may have bought goods on credit, in which case they are a trade payable and owe money for the goods received.

The accounting equation

Assets = Owner's equity + Liabilities

This equation shows that the assets of the business are always equal to the owner's equity and liabilities. If one element is missing you can calculate it using the other two elements.

Follow the example below to see that the equation always balances:

June 1 Jiao set up as a fitness instructor. She opened a business bank account and paid $5 000 in as capital
 2 The business purchased sound equipment for $1 000, and paid by cheque
 3 The business purchased clothing to sell to clients, $2 200, on credit
 4 The business purchased yoga mats to use in classes, $800, and paid by cheque

Show the accounting equation after each of the above transactions.

Date	Assets		= Owner's equity	+ Liabilities
June 1	Bank	$50 000	$50 000	Nil
2	Equipment	1 000		Nil
	Bank	49 000		
		$50 000		
3	Equipment	1 000		
	Inventory	2 200		
	Bank	49 000		
		$52 200	$50 000	Trade payable $2 200
4	Equipment	1 800		
	Inventory	2 200		
	Bank	48 200		
		$52 200	$50 000	Trade payable $2 200

June 1 Jiao has paid $50 000 into the business bank account which increases both the assets of the business and the owner's equity.

 2 The money in the bank has decreased because the sound equipment, which is an assets, has been purchased. The total assets still equal the owner's equity.

 3 Buying goods on credit means that Jiao has a chance to sell them on to her clients before the date she needs to pay. This means her asset of inventory increases and so do her liabilities as she now owes money to the credit supplier who is a trade payable.

4   The yoga mats are to be used by the business so will be included in the asset of equipment. The bank was used to make the payment so the asset of equipment will increase and the asset of bank will decrease. The total assets are equal to the owner's equity plus liabilities.

The statement of financial position

The accounting equation forms the basis of the statement of financial position. It shows the assets of the business, what it owns or has owed to it, and the liabilities, what the business owes and what the owner has contributed in terms of assets (owner's equity). In the same way that the accounting equation always balances, the statement of financial position must too.

Sample questions

1   Calculate the missing amounts:

Assets $	Owner's equity $	Liabilities $
150 000	100 000	
	84 000	35 000
48 000		22 500

Answer:

Assets $	Owner's equity $	Liabilities $
150 000	100 000	50 000
119 000	84 000	35 000
48 000	25 500	22 500

2   A business may employ both a book-keeper and an accountant. What is the role of the book-keeper?

A   to make financial decisions about the business's future

B   to prepare income statements at regular intervals

C   to record all the financial transactions of the business

D   to summarise the assets and liabilities of the business

Answer: The answer is C. The book-keeper could be involved in all sorts of aspects of a business and its finances. However, their primary role is to record all the financial transactions of the business. This information is then used by the accountant to produce financial statements.

3   State whether each item is an asset or liability by ticking next to each item the category in which it belongs:

	Asset	Liability
Motor vehicle		
Bank overdraft		
Trade payables		
Trade receivables		

Answer:

	Asset	Liability
Motor vehicle	✓	
Bank overdraft		✓
Trade payables		✓
Trade receivables	✓	

> **TIPS**
>
> Think of assets as being positive items you would be happy to have. Liabilities aren't necessarily bad, as often a business needs to borrow to expand, but on a personal level you would rather have lots of assets and few liabilities.
>
> Owner's equity isn't necessarily just cash or bank amounts introduced by the owner. It could be equipment or a motor vehicle. This can increase throughout the business's life depending on what the owner's plans are and does not just happen at the start of the business.

Progress check

1. What is the difference between book-keeping and accounting?
2. State the accounting equation.
3. Define assets, liabilities and owner's equity.
4. What does a statement of financial position show?

Examination-style questions

1. What is the purpose of accounting? [1]
   A to check the bank statement
   B to control trade receivables
   C to ensure all financial transactions are recorded
   D to prepare financial statements

2. Give one example of an asset. [1]

3. Prepare the following table to show the effect of each of the following transactions. [6]
   The first one has been completed as an example.

   a Bought equipment and paid by cash
   b Received a loan into the bank account
   c Bought property using a loan
   d Sold goods for cash

	Effect on assets	$	Effect on liabilities	$
a	Equipment Cash	Increase Decrease	No effect	
b				
c				
d				

4 A simplified statement of financial position of Meera Traders on 31 May 20–9 is shown below.

Meera Traders
Statement of financial position at 31 May 20–9

	$
Assets	
Property	160 000
Equipment	12 500
Inventory	3 300
Trade receivables	2 800
Bank	6 200
Cash	450
	185 250
Capital and liabilities	
Owner's equity	128 380
Liabilities	
Bank loan	50 000
Trade payables	6 870
	185 250

On 1 June 20–9 the following transactions took place:

- Repaid $2 000 bank loan by cheque.
- Paid a credit supplier $90 in cash.
- Received a cheque from a credit customer for $125.
- Bought goods on credit for $140.

Prepare the statement of financial position of Meera Traders on 1 June 20–9 after the above transactions have taken place. [11]

5 A business provided the following information:

	$
Property	125 000
Inventory	32 500
Trade payables	8 430
Bank overdraft	2 200
Cash	125
Machinery	12 600
Delivery van	5 800

a Calculate the value of the assets. [1]

b Calculate the value of the liabilities. [1]

c Use the accounting equation to calculate the owner's equity. [1]

Revision checklist

In this chapter you have learnt:

- [ ] the difference between book-keeping, recording financial transactions and accounting which uses the book-keeping records to prepare financial statements and to assist in decision-making

- [ ] the purpose of measuring business profit and loss is so that a business owner can makes plans according to the outcomes

- [ ] the role of accounting in providing information for monitoring progress and decision-making

- [ ] the meaning of assets, which represent items owned by or owing to the business; liabilities, which represent anything owed by the business; and owner's equity, which is also known as capital and is what the business owes to the owner

- [ ] the accounting equation which is Assets – Liabilities = Owner's equity or capital

- [ ] that statements of financial position record assets and liabilities on a specified date and also show the owner's equity.

Double entry book-keeping – Part A

Chapter 2

Learning summary

By the end of this chapter you should understand:

- an outline of the double entry system of book-keeping
- how to process accounting data using the double entry system
- how to prepare ledger accounts
- how to post transactions to the ledger accounts
- how to balance ledger accounts as required
- how to interpret ledger accounts and their balances.

TERMS

A balance on a ledger account is the difference between the debit side and the credit side.

Carriage is the cost of transporting goods. Carriage inwards is the cost of bringing the goods to the business and carriage outwards is the cost of delivering the goods to the customer.

Double entry book-keeping is the process of making a debit entry and a credit entry for each transaction.

Drawings represent any value taken from the business by the owner of that business. It could be in the form of money, non-current assets or inventory.

Purpose of the double entry system of book-keeping

A concept which you may not have considered prior to studying accounting is that every financial transaction actually has two outcomes. For example, if you travel by bus to your place of study you are losing your asset of money in return for the bus travel. If you buy some lunch in the canteen you are losing the asset of money and gaining the asset of food. The business records each transaction in ledger accounts for each type of asset, expense, liability, income and each trade receivable and trade payable.

A ledger was originally a large bound book but nowadays even the smallest of businesses will use a computer system which acts in a similar manner. It keeps track of every financial transaction. One account will be debited and the other credited. You cannot debit both accounts or credit both accounts. The rules are debit the account which gains value, or records an asset or an expense, and credit the account which gives value, or records a liability or an income item.

Accounts	To record	Entry in the account
Assets	An increase	Debit
	A decrease	Credit
Liabilities	An increase	Credit
	A decrease	Debit
Capital	An increase	Credit
	A decrease	Debit

Sample question

1.
   20–8

   Feb 1   Pari opened her business and deposited $65 000 in the business bank account as owner's equity

        2   A delivery van was purchased for $12 000 and was paid by cheque

        4   A long term loan was received from the bank for $10 000

        5   Computer equipment costing $5 500 was purchased by cheque

Prepare Pari's ledger by entering these transactions.

Answer:

Pari
Bank account

Date	Details	$	Date	Details	$
20–8			20–8		
Feb 1	Capital	65 000	Feb 2	Delivery van	12 000
4	Bank loan	10 000	5	Computer equipment	5 500

Capital account

Date	Details	$	Date	Details	$
			20–8		
			Feb 1	Bank	65 000

Delivery van account

Date	Details	$	Date	Details	$
20–8					
Feb 2	Bank	12 000			

Bank loan account

Date	Details	$	Date	Details	$
			20–8		
			Feb 4	Bank	10 000

Computer equipment account

Date	Details	$	Date	Details	$
20–8					
Feb 5	Bank	5 500			

> **TIPS**
>
> You can abbreviate months in ledger accounts. Dates are very important in ledger accounts and if a date column in supplied in the question you should always use it.
>
> Many transactions involve bank or cash items. To help you remember the double entry just think money comes in on the debit side and out on the credit side. If you do the entry which involves the bank or cash first it is much easier to work out the opposing entry.
>
> The word 'goods' should not be used in ledger accounts. Goods are either purchased, sold or returned and each movement of goods has its own account.
>
> Carriage inwards and carriage outwards are both types of delivery expenses so are both debited. They are not the opposite of each other like sales returns and purchases returns.

Sample question

2

20–9		
Apr 1	Jamil received $6 600 from his tenant for rent received by cheque	
2	He paid wages of $480 by cheque	
4	He paid motor expenses of $230 by cheque	

Enter these transactions in Jamil's ledger.

Answer:

Jamil
Bank account

Date	Details	$	Date	Details	$
20–9					
Apr 1	Rent received	6 600	Apr 2	Wages	480
			4	Motor expenses	230

Rent received account

Date	Details	$	Date	Details	$
			20–9		
			Apr 1	Bank	6 600

Wages account

Date	Details	$	Date	Details	$
20–9					
Apr 2	Bank	480			

Motor expenses account

Date	Details	$	Date	Details	$
20–9					
Apr 4	Bank	230			

Double entry records for drawings

A drawings account is used to collect transactions where the owner has taken money, non-current assets or inventory for their own use. This account is debited each time and the corresponding account is credited. At the end of the financial year the total from this ledger account is subtracted from the capital section on the statement of financial position. This is because the owner has effectively reduced the amount they have invested in the business by removing amounts.

Balancing ledger accounts

Balancing off a ledger account is an important skill to learn and practice. Balancing off a ledger account provides essential information, such as how much we have spent in total on advertising, how much a trade receivable owes us or how much money we have in our bank account.

This is done in five stages:

1 Add up both sides to find their totals. Do not write anything in the account at this stage.

2 Deduct the smaller total from the larger total to find the balance.

3 Now enter the balance on the side with the smallest total. This now means the totals will be equal.

4 Enter totals on a level with each other, then add lines above and below, and double underline.

5 Now enter the balance on the line below the totals. The balance below the totals should be the opposite side to the balance shown above the totals.

Against the balance above the totals, complete the date column by showing the last day of that period. Below the totals show the first day of the next period against the balance. The balance above the totals is described as balance **carried down**. The balance below the total is described as balance **brought down**.

Sample question 3

Pari
Bank account

Date	Details	$	Date	Details	$
20–8			20–8		
Feb 1	Capital	65 000	Feb 2	Delivery van	12 000
4	Bank loan	10 000	5	Computer equipment	5 500

Balance the bank account in Pari's books on 5 February 20–8.

Answer:

Pari
Bank account

Date	Details	$	Date	Details	$
20–8			20–8		
Feb 1	Capital	65 000	Feb 2	Delivery van	12 000
4	Bank loan	10 000	5	Computer equipment	5 500
			5	Balance c/d	57 500
		75 000			75 000
6	Balance b/d	57 500			

Start by finding the side with the highest total; in this case it is the debit side with $75 000. Insert this amount on both sides and then subtract the other entries on the credit side, which total $17 500, to find the closing balance of $57 500 which is then brought down as the opening balance for the next day. Note how the date moves on to the next day for the balance brought down.

Double entry for sales, purchases and returns

Separate accounts are kept for each different type of movement of inventory for sales, purchases, sales returns and purchases returns. Cash sales and purchases which include payment using the bank account only require two entries for the transaction.

	Sales	Purchases
Debit	Bank or cash account	Purchases
Credit	Sales	Bank or cash account

It is important to write cash or bank but not both.

Credit sales and purchases require four transactions; two for the movement of goods and two for the receipt of the money. Even though the business has not yet received the money the transaction still counts towards sales and purchases and, subsequently, profit.

	Movement of goods			Receipt of money	
	Sales	Purchases		Sales	Purchases
Debit	Trade receivable	Purchases	Debit	Bank or cash	Trade payable
Credit	Sales	Trade payable	Credit	Trade receivable	Bank or cash

Sales returns occurs when sales of inventory we have made are returned to us. This could be because the customer has over-ordered or goods are faulty. We debit sales returns as it is the opposite to making a sale which is a credit, and then credit the customer. This amount will eventually be deducted from sales but we need to keep a separate account until we produce the financial statements.

Purchases returns is used when we return purchases of inventory for the same sort of reasons that customers may return goods to us. This time we debit the supplier and credit the purchases returns account. This will be deducted from purchases in the income statement.

If you return a non-current asset, it is credited to the non-current asset account, it does not go into purchases returns.

Sample question

4 Enter the following transactions in the ledger of Pari.

> 20–8
> Feb 8   Pari bought goods for $350 on credit from Russell & Co
> 9   Pari sold goods for $500 and received a cheque
> 10   She returns goods worth $50 to Russell & Co
> 11   She sells goods on credit to Rogue Traders for $125
> 12   She pays Russell & Co the amount owing by cheque

Answer:

Pari
Russell & Co account

Date	Details	$	Date	Details	$
20–8			20–8		
Feb 10	Purchases returns	50	Feb 8	Purchases	350
12	Bank	300			
		350			350

Pari has settled her account with Russell & Co so there is no closing balance on this account. To work out how much she needed to pay on 12 February, the purchases returns was subtracted from the purchases.

Purchases account

Date	Details	$	Date	Details	$
20–8					
Feb 8	Russell & Co	350			

Bank account

Date	Details	$	Date	Details	$
20–8					
Feb 9	Sales	500			

Sales account

Date	Details	$	Date	Details	$
			20–8		
			Feb 9	Bank	500
			11	Rogue Traders	125

Purchases returns account

Date	Details	$	Date	Details	$
			20–8		
			Feb 10	Russell & Co	50

Rogue Traders account

Date	Details	$	Date	Details	$
20–8					
Feb 11	Sales	125			

Double entry for carriage inwards and carriage outwards

Carriage inwards and carriage outwards are both types of delivery expenses so the double entry is to debit the carriage inwards or outwards account and then credit either cash or bank depending on the method of payment. Carriage inwards is when the business pays to have purchases delivered to them, and carriage outwards is paying for delivery of sales to customers.

Interpreting ledger accounts and their balances

If there is an opening debit balance on an expense account then this means that a prepayment has been made, the expense has been paid ahead of when it should have been. An opening credit balance on an expense account means that the expense is owing (an accrual). If the account is an income account then it works the opposite way, so if a trade receivable has paid early or paid a deposit, it does not belong to the business and is represented as a credit on the ledger account. The business effectively owes the trade receivable. If an income is owed to the business (for example rent received), then this appears as a debit balance. Remember that every debit entry results in a credit entry and the label of the entry is the name of the opposite account involved.

Progress check

1. Why does every transaction have both a debit and credit entry?
2. What form can drawings take other than cash?
3. What effect do drawings have on the capital account at the end of the financial year?
4. How does the double entry differ when selling goods on credit rather than for cash?

Examination-style questions

1. State how Sandra would record the sale of goods on credit to Imran. [2]

Account debited	Account credited

2. Chen supplies plumbing equipment and has just started his business. He provides the following information:

20–8	
Apr 1	Chen paid $20 000 capital into the business bank account
2	Bought a delivery van for $3 500 and paid by cheque
3	Bought goods on credit from Leak and Sons for $4 400
4	Returned $200 worth of goods to Leak and Sons as they were faulty
4	Paid rent of $1 500 by cheque
5	Sold goods for $350 cash
6	Paid wages of $120 by cash
7	Sold goods on credit to Paul's Plumbers for $2 050

Prepare the ledger of Chen by entering these transactions. Balance all of the accounts with more than one transaction on 7 April and bring down the balances on 8 April 20–8. [24]

3   Medi is a trader. On 1 September 20–9 she had the following balances in her ledger:

	$
Capital	13 000
Motor vehicle	4 200
Machinery	12 500
Trade receivable – Lola	1 890
Trade payable – Noah	1 650
Loan from Lend It Finance	4 200
Bank	260 debit

a Prepare the appropriate ledger accounts by entering the above balances. [7]

The following transactions took place in September 20–9:

Sept 3	Bought goods on credit from Noah for $2 200
4	Returned goods to Noah, $125
8	Sold goods for $5 600 and paid the money directly into the bank
15	Paid $1 000 to Lend It Finance by cheque
21	Lola returned damaged goods, $200
22	Lola paid the amount due by cheque
23	Took $100 from the bank for her own use
30	Bought machinery on credit from Moriarty Ltd for $4 050

b Prepare Medi's ledger by entering these transactions. Balance all accounts, with more than one transaction and bring down the balances on 1 October 20–9. [24]

4   Give the name of each account to be debited or credited. The first one has been completed as an example. [16]

Transaction	Debit	Credit
Rent paid with cash	Rent	Cash
Goods for resale purchased from Lomax on credit		
Cash sales		
Wages paid by cheque		
Purchase of machinery by cheque		
Goods for resale purchased from Logan with cash		
Vehicle service paid by cheque		
Drawings of cash		
Purchase of vehicle on credit from Daunt		

5 Marie purchased goods for resale on credit from Nathan.

Which entries would Marie make in her ledger? [1]

	Account to be debited	Account to be credited
A	Bank	Purchases
B	Nathan	Purchases
C	Purchases	Bank
D	Purchases	Nathan

Revision checklist

In this chapter you have learnt:

- ☐ an outline of the double entry system of book-keeping – these are the building blocks to the accounting system

- ☐ how to process accounting data using the double entry system – for every debit entry there is a corresponding credit entry

- ☐ how to prepare ledger accounts

- ☐ how to post transactions to the ledger accounts remembering dates and the name of the corresponding account

- ☐ how to balance ledger accounts as required – find the highest total and then subtract the amounts from the other side of the ledger

- ☐ how to interpret ledger accounts and their balances – opening balances for expenses, assets and drawings are debit, and for liabilities, income and capital items are credit.

The trial balance

Chapter 3

Learning summary

By the end of this chapter you should understand:

- that a trial balance is a statement of ledger balances on a particular date
- the uses and limitations of a trial balance
- how to prepare a trial balance from a given list of balances and amend a trial balance which contains errors
- how to identify and explain those errors which do not affect the trial balance – commission, compensating, complete reversal, omission, original entry and principle.

TERMS

A compensating error is when two or more errors cancel each other out.

An error of commission is when the wrong name of the account is used in the correct ledger.

An error of complete reversal is when an account is debited instead of credited and vice versa.

An error of omission is when an entry has been completely missed out of the ledger accounts.

An error of original entry is when there is an incorrect figure in both ledger accounts.

An error of principle is when the wrong type or class of account is used.

The trial balance is a list of balances on the accounts in the ledger at a certain date.

Purpose and uses of a trial balance

A trial balance is a list of all account ledger balances on a particular date sorted according to whether they are a debit or credit balance. For every debit entry in a ledger account there must be a credit entry, so if we have carried out our double entry correctly then the totals of the two columns should match. The balances can then be used to prepare the income statement and the statement of financial position.

Layout for a trial balance

The title for a trial balance is at a certain date as the next day balances will change again.

Trial balance for E. Watt at 30 June 20–8

	Debit $	Credit $
Revenue		70 000
Purchases	50 000	
Electricity	2 000	
Wages	1 600	
Drawings	3 300	
Cash and cash equivalents	125 000	
Trade receivables	42 000	
Trade payables		22 000
Owner's equity		131 900
	223 900	223 900

The items which appear in the debit column are assets, expenses or drawings and the items in the credit column are liabilities, any type of income, including revenue and capital, or the equity section for a limited company.

Accounts that will have debit balances	Accounts that will have credit balances
Debit	**C**redit
Expenses	**L**iabilities
Assets	**I**ncome/revenue
Drawings = **DEAD**	**C**apital (owner's equity) = **CLIC**
Expenses	Income, i.e. interest received, rent received
Purchases	Purchases returns
Sales returns	Revenue
Inventory	Loans
Non-current assets	Trade payables
Trade receivables	Bank overdraft
Cash and cash equivalents	Owner's equity
Drawings	Capital accounts for partnerships

Errors which cause a trial balance not to balance

There are several reasons why your trial balance may not balance at first so you need to check through the following:

1. A ledger account has been incorrectly balanced off or missed off the trial balance.
2. A debit entry has been made in a ledger account without the corresponding credit entry.

3 A transaction has been entered on the wrong side of one ledger account but the correct side elsewhere.

4 Re-check the addition of both columns of the trial balance. Find out which column has the highest value and then subtract the other column's value to find the missing account balance.

A trial balance with errors

Trial balance for Zara for the year ended 31 December 20–7

	Debit $	Credit $
Revenue	250 000	
Purchases	130 000	
Operating expenses	22 000	
Motor vehicles		120 000
Purchases returns		6 000
Cash and cash equivalents	2 500	
Owner's equity		100 000
Drawings		6 000
	404 500	232 000

The errors in the trial balance are as follows:

a The title should be 'at' as the balances are correct for one day only.

b Revenue should be in the credit column as it is money received.

c The ledger account for purchases was incorrectly balanced and should be $120 000.

d Motor vehicles are an asset so should be in the debit column.

e Trade receivables of $25 500 is missing from the trial balance.

f Drawings of $6 000 was recorded in the wrong column. Drawings are the opposite of owner's equity so need to be in the debit column.

Corrected trial balance for Zara at 31 December 20–7

	Debit $	Credit $
Revenue		250 000
Purchases	180 000	
Operating expenses	22 000	
Motor vehicles	120 000	
Purchases returns		6 000
Cash and cash equivalents	2 500	
Owner's equity		100 000
Trade receivables	25 500	
Drawings	6 000	
	356 000	356 000

Limitations of the trial balance

The trial balance is only as accurate as the information it gathers from the ledger accounts so it is possible to believe you have a correct set of balances whilst there are actually hidden errors.

Errors that will not be revealed by the trial balance

The following errors are hidden as the trial balance will still balance; the total debits will equal the total credits.

Error of commission – this is where the correct type of ledger but the wrong account name is used. For example, mixing up two trade receivable names, such as D. Shaw and J. Shore. This can also apply to mixing up similar types of expenses, for example, car insurance and car repairs.

Compensating error – if one account with a debit balance is overstated (is too high) and another with a credit balance is also overstated by the same amount, then the two errors will cancel each other out and the trial balance will still balance.

Error of complete reversal – if a credit sale is debited rather than credited and the trade receivable is credited instead of debited, then this is a complete reversal and the error will not be revealed in the trial balance.

Error of omission – this is a very common error as it involves completely forgetting to enter a transaction. It could be a misplaced electricity bill or a receipt that is missing. Because the entry is missing, this will not show up on the trial balance as it will still balance.

Error of original entry – this is when the same wrong amount is entered in both accounts. For example, debiting the electricity account $47 and crediting the bank account $47 when both entries should be $74.

Error of principle – this final error involves using the wrong category or type of account. For example, purchasing a non-current asset, such as equipment, and placing it into the purchases account.

> **TIPS**
>
> If your trial balance does not balance, check the difference between the debit and credit column and see if you can spot the same amount in the information you have been provided to see if you have missed an entry out.
>
> Always re-check your additions of both the debit and credit columns. It is easy to make a silly error.
>
> If an error is incorrect in both accounts then it is one of our six hidden errors. If just one entry is incorrect then a suspense account is required – see Chapter 4.
>
> You could be asked to complete a trial balance for a partnership or a limited company. It works in the same way; just remember that capital is also a credit when contributed by partners or by shareholders.
>
> Remember that carriage inwards and carriage outwards are both types of expenses so are both debit entries.

Progress check

1. What is a trial balance?
2. How can a trial balance still balance and yet include errors?
3. State and give examples of the six errors which do not affect the trial balance.
4. What are the uses and limitations of a trial balance?

Sample questions

1. Vera is new to accounting and is very happy to discover her trial balance balances; all the debits are equal to the credits. Her friend Rashid believes that there could still be mistakes.

   Explain why there could still be mistakes in the trial balance.

   Answer: A trial balance is simply a list of ledger account balances and if there is an error in the ledger accounts then this will be transferred to the trial balance. For example, error of omission means that the entire transaction is missing from the accounting records, such as a misplaced invoice. You can use any of the six errors to illustrate your answer.

2. Which statement describes the purpose of a trial balance?

   A It calculates profit or loss for the year.

   B It checks the arithmetical accuracy of the double entry.

   C It prevents errors in the ledger accounts.

   D It stops errors in the books of prime entry.

   Answer: The answer is B – The purpose of a trial balance is to check the arithmetical accuracy of the double entry.

3. Sioux made a payment to Joe, a credit supplier. In error she debited the account of Jason.

   Which type of error did Sioux make?

   A commission B omission C original entry D principle

   Answer: The answer is A as Joe and Jason are both credit suppliers. The entry is in the correct ledger but the wrong name of the account which has been used.

4. Complete the following table, indicating with a tick whether each account would appear on the debit side or the credit side of a trial balance.

	Debit side	Credit side
Equipment		
Trade payables		
Revenue		
Carriage outwards		
Discount allowed		
Wages and salaries		
Rent received		
Drawings		

Answer:

	Debit side	Credit side
Equipment	✓	
Trade payables		✓
Revenue		✓
Carriage outwards	✓	
Discount allowed	✓	
Wages and salaries	✓	
Rent received		✓
Drawings	✓	

Examination-style questions

1 The following trial balance has been compiled by an inexperienced book-keeper who cannot understand why the total of the debit column does not equal the total of the credit column.

   Prepare a revised trial balance with all items in the correct columns. [10].

   Trial balance for Sandeep at 31 July 20–8

	Debit $	Credit $
Rent received	10 500	
Carriage inwards		525
Carriage outwards	375	
Revenue		235 720
Purchases		111 340
Sales returns	3 245	
Purchases returns	6 211	
Wages and salaries	32 895	
Insurance		3 190
Cash and cash equivalents	2 200	
Fixtures and fittings	22 490	
Sundry expenses	4 498	
Inventory at 1 August 20–8		4 390
Drawings	22 500	
Owner's equity	25 000	
Property at cost	78 779	
	208 693	355 165

2 Keung's new book-keeper has prepared all the ledger account balances and is unsure how to prepare a trial balance. Use the following balances to prepare a trial balance for Keung at 30 April 20–8. [12]

Details	$
Bank overdraft	2 300
Bank loan	4 500
Owner's equity	52 000
Revenue	369 000
Purchases	152 500
Returns inwards	2 220
Returns outwards	480
Property	180 000
Motor vehicles	99 000
Wages and salaries	33 000
Trade receivables	4 855
Trade payables	3 354
Rent and rates	5 600
Drawings	12 000
Inventory at 1 May 20–7	8 459

3 Identify the error for each of the following situations: [4]

   a A purchase of a new delivery van is recorded in purchases.

   b A sales invoice has been mislaid and not recorded.

c The motor insurance account has been debited instead of the vehicle repairs account.

d The sales account has been overcast by $350 and the general expenses has been overcast by $350.

4 Explain two reasons for the trial balance not to balance. [2]

5 After preparing the trial balance, Zeena discovered the following errors:

a Goods bought on credit from Tsz, $840, had not been recorded in the books.

b A sale of goods to Bilal, $75, had been recorded in the account of Bilom.

c A purchase of computer equipment had been recorded as cash purchases.

d Discount received from Taylor had been credited to his account and debited to the discount received account.

Give the name of the type of error in each of **a** to **d**. [4]

Error	Type of error
a	
b	
c	
d	

6 Polly returned goods on credit to a supplier and debited purchases returns and credited the supplier.

Which type of error did Polly make? [1]

A commission   C original entry

B complete reversal   D principle

Revision checklist

In this chapter you have learnt:

- how to compile a trial balance from a list of ledger account balances on a particular date using DEAD CLIC to remind you which side to place the amount

- the uses and limitations of a trial balance

- how to prepare a trial balance from a given list of balances and amend a trial balance which contains errors

- that there are errors which do not affect the trial balance which are errors of commission, compensating, complete reversal, omission, original entry and principle

- that these errors are hidden and mean that the total debit balances will still equal the total credit balances.

Chapter 4

Double entry book-keeping – Part B

Learning summary

By the end of this chapter you should understand:

- the division of the ledger into the sales ledger, the purchases ledger and the nominal (general) ledger
- the use of, and be able to process, accounting information in the cash book
- how to distinguish between, and account for, trade discount and cash discounts
- the dual function of the cash book as a book of prime entry and as a ledger account for bank and cash
- the use of, and be able to record, payments and receipts made by bank transfers and other electronic means.

TERMS

A **bank overdraft** occurs when more has been paid out of the bank than was put into the bank account.

Cash discount is an allowance given to a customer when an account is settled within a time limit set by the supplier.

A **contra entry** is one which appears on both sides of the cash book.

A **dishonoured cheque** is a cheque received which the trade receivable's bank refuses to pay, often due to insufficient funds.

Nominal (general) ledger is the ledger where all other accounts are maintained.

Purchases ledger is the ledger in which the accounts of credit suppliers are maintained.

Sales ledger is the ledger in which the accounts of credit customers are maintained.

Trade discount is a negotiated reduction in the price of goods and is not recorded in the accounting records, unlike cash discount.

Division of the ledger

All financial transactions of a business using a double entry book-keeping system are recorded in the ledger. In a small business, it may be possible to use only one ledger. From a practical point of view, it makes sense for a larger business to separate parts of the ledger according to the entries and this allows the work to be divided amongst several people.

Cash books: since the bank and cash accounts are used more frequently than any other accounts, they are kept in a separate area for the cash book and petty cash book.

Sales ledger: where all credit customers are kept and this is also known as the trade receivables ledger.

Purchases ledger: where all credit suppliers are kept and this is also known as the trade payables ledger.

Nominal (or general) ledger: where all the remaining accounts are kept. This includes accounts of assets, liabilities, expenses, incomes, sales, purchases and returns.

The two column cash book

The two column cash book combines both the cash and bank account together. They still have to be balanced off separately, and it is possible for the bank to have a credit balance (overdraft) or a debit balance whilst the cash must always have a debit balance. As well as being part of the double entry system, the cash book is also a book of prime entry. Money paid into either account is a debit entry and money out is a credit entry.

Often there are entries which concern both the cash and bank account and these are called contra entries. For example, at the end of a day the business may not want to keep too much cash in the office or shop and so pay it into the bank. This would reduce the cash account (credit) and increase the bank account (debit). Or perhaps cash is needed to pay the weekly wages, so in this case the cash will be withdrawn from the bank and so the cash account will increase (debit) and the bank account will decrease (credit). The letter 'c' is usually written next to the account name to represent the contra entry.

Over the years there has been a move away from the traditional payments using cash and cheque towards electronic means. These ways are often quicker and more secure. Credit transfers can either come into or out of a business and involve the money moving directly from one bank account to another. Both standing orders and direct debits are types of payments but it is who controls them that is important. With a standing order it is the person making the payment who controls it, it is suitable for regular payments such as rent and the bank is instructed to pay the fixed amount at fixed intervals to another person. Direct debits, however, hand control over to the person collecting the money and are recurring payments, but amounts may vary, for example, mobile phone payments. Debit cards are connected to the bank account, whereas a credit card is operated by a card company and the person with the credit card owes that company the money and can either pay some or all of the money owing back each month.

Sample question

1 Hetty maintains a two column cash book. The following transactions have taken place:

> 20–7
> Oct 1 Hetty starts her business paying $5 000 of capital into the bank account
>   2 Purchased goods by cheque, $2 400
>   3 Cash sales, $2 380
>   3 Stationery purchased, $120 cash
>   4 Paid advertising expenses, $48 by cheque
>   5 $1,950 cash paid into bank
>   5 Cash sales paid directly into bank, $2 785
>   6 Standing order for rent of $490
>   7 Cash withdrawn from bank, $2 500
>   7 Wages paid, $1 988 cash

Prepare the two-column cash book for Hetty by entering these transactions. Balance the cash book on 7 October 20–7.

Answer:

Date	Details	Cash $	Bank $	Date	Details	Cash $	Bank $
20–7				20–7			
Oct 1	Capital		5 000	Oct 2	Purchases		2 400
3	Sales	2 380		3	Stationery	120	
5	Cash c		1 950	4	Advertising		48
5	Sales		2 785	5	Bank c	1 950	
7	Bank c	2 500		6	Rent payable		490
				7	Cash c		2 500
				7	Wages	1 988	
				7	Balance c/d	822	4 297
		4 880	9 735			4 880	9 735
8	Balance b/d	822	4 297				

The three column cash book

The quicker that customers settle their bills the better. To encourage swift payment some firms may offer a reduction in the amount owed, known as a cash discount. It is still called this even if payment is by cheque or credit transfer via the bank. Full details of the percentage allowed, and the period within which payment is to be made, are quoted on the sales documents.

A discount allowed is when a business gives its credit customers a discount for paying early. It is an expense to the business and reduces profit but it helps with the cash situation. In the same way, the business itself may gain a cash discount from credit suppliers and this is a discount received that will be added to gross profit. These discounts are recorded in the third column of the cash book. The discount allowed is on the debit side and discount received on the credit side. These columns are then simply totalled at the end of the period and their totals transferred to the double entry system.

Cash discounts are different to a trade discount as trade discounts are not recorded in the accounting system. Trade discounts may be linked to how loyal a customer is, how much they buy and so on, and is simply a way of negotiating a better price than perhaps less frequent buyers would receive.

A dishonoured cheque occurs when the bank refuses to pay for the cheque which is presented to it. This could be due to insufficient funds in the account or an error on the cheque, such as the figure and amount in words not matching, or there being no signature or no date. The business needs to record this by crediting the bank account because otherwise it will think it has more money in the account than it actually has. It is important to then chase up this amount with the trade receivable concerned.

> **TIPS**
>
> When recording a contra entry the account name needs to be where the money is going to or coming from, so, if you are taking money from the bank and putting it into cash, the credit side will state 'cash' for details and the debit side will state 'bank'.
>
> Do not balance off discount columns in a three column cash book; simply total them to then transfer to the appropriate ledger account.
>
> You must label a dishonoured cheque as 'bank' in the trade receivable's account. Remember it is the name of the other account involved and not the action which has caused the entry.

Progress check

1. What is the difference between a two and a three column cash book?
2. How can the opening balance for the bank column be a credit?
3. What can cause a cheque to be dishonoured by the bank?
4. What is the difference between a direct debit and a standing order?

Sample question

2 Caiden maintains a three column cash book and divides the ledger into three sections – sales ledger, purchases ledger and nominal ledger. Balance the cash book on 30 November 20–6 and transfer the totals of the discount columns to the relevant accounts in the nominal ledger. Balance the accounts in the sales and purchases ledger where necessary.

20–6		
Nov 1	Caiden had a cash balance of $320 and a bank overdraft of $600
2	Sold goods on credit to N Gallagher for $330
3	Bought goods on credit from HCC Ltd for $950
6	Received a cheque from N Gallagher for $200
8	Sold goods on credit to B Buckley for $800
9	N Gallagher's cheque was dishonoured and returned by the bank
10	Cash sales, $805
11	Paid wages in cash, $150
12	Paid $220 cash into the bank account
13	B Buckley paid the amount due by credit transfer after deducting a cash discount of 5%
22	Paid insurance, $120, by standing order
28	Paid HCC Ltd the amount due by credit transfer after deducting a discount of 4%

Answer:

Caiden
Sales ledger
N Gallagher account

Date	Details	$	Date	Details	$
20–6			20–6		
Nov 2	Sales	330	Nov 6	Bank	200
9	Bank (dishonoured cheque)	200	30	Balance c/d	330
		550			550
Dec 1	Balance b/d	330			

B Buckley account

Date	Details	$	Date	Details	$
20–6			20–6		
Nov 8	Sales	800	Nov 13	Bank	760
				Discount allowed	40
		800			800

Purchases ledger
HCC Ltd account

Date	Details	$	Date	Details	$
20–6			20–6		
Nov 28	Bank	912	Nov 3	Purchases	950
	Discount received	38			
		950			950

Nominal ledger
Purchases account

Date	Details	$	Date	Details	$
20–6					
Nov 3	HCC Ltd	950			

Sales account

Date	Details	$	Date	Details	$
			20–6		
			Nov 2	N Gallagher	330
			8	B Buckley	800
			10	Cash	805

Wages account

Date	Details	$	Date	Details	$
20–6					
Nov 11	Cash	150			

Insurance account

Date	Details	$	Date	Details	$
20–6					
Nov 22	Bank	120			

Discount allowed account

Date	Details	$	Date	Details	$
20–6					
Nov 30	Total for month	40			

Discount received account

Date	Details	$	Date	Details	$
			20–6		
			Nov 30	Total for month	38

Cash book

Date	Details	Discount allowed $	Cash $	Bank $	Date	Details	Discount received $	Cash $	Bank $
20–6					20–6				
Nov 1	Balance b/d		320		Nov 1	Balance b/d			600
6	N Gallagher			200	9	N Gallagher			200
8	Sales		805		11	Wages		150	
12	Cash c			220	12	Bank c		220	
13	B Buckley	40		760	22	Insurance			120
					28	HCC Ltd	38		912
30	Balance c/d			652	30	Balance c/d		755	
		40	1 125	1 832			38	1 125	1 832
Dec 1	Balance b/d		755		Dec 1	Balance b/d			652

Examination-style questions

1 Raju's cash book had a debit balance of $300. When the bank statement arrived he saw that a customer's cheque for $160 had been dishonoured, and he had received $10 in bank interest.

What was the balance on the cash book when it had been updated? [1]

A $130 debit

B $150 debit

C $450 credit

D $470 credit

2 Prepare the following table, giving the name of the ledger in which each account appears. The first one has been completed as an example. [5]

Account	Ledger
Machinery	*Nominal*
Becca, a credit customer	
Purchases	
Carriage outwards	
Luke, a credit supplier	
Drawings	

3 Zeena is a trader who buys and sells on cash and credit terms. She provided the following information for March 20–9:

Mar 1	Ted, a credit customer, owed Zeena, $2 200.
8	Ted purchased goods on credit from Zeena, list price $1 200, less 20% trade discount.
12	Ted returned to Zeena some of the goods purchased on 8 March, list price $100.
24	Ted paid the balance owed to Zeena at 1 March by credit transfer and was allowed 5% cash discount.

a Prepare the account of Ted in the ledger of Zeena for March 20–9. Balance the account and bring down the balance on 1 April 20–9. [5]

b State the subdivision of Zeena's ledger which would contain the account of Ted. [1]

4 Noah maintains a full set of accounting records, including a three column cash book. He provided the following information for September 20–9:

Sept 1	Cash $230, bank $8 120 credit
	Trade receivables – Simon $520
	Trade payables – Rachel $960
4	Bought fixtures and fittings for $326 by cheque
8	Paid Rachel by credit transfer in settlement of her account less 5% discount
13	Cash sales, $2 380
14	Noah took $50 cash for personal use
16	Received a cheque from Simon for $500 in full settlement of his account
20	Paid $78 electricity by direct debit
23	Paid $890 rent by standing order
24	The cheque received from Simon was returned dishonoured
25	Paid wages in cash of $400
28	Simon paid $500 by credit transfer
30	Paid all cash into the bank except $150

a Prepare the accounts by entering the balances in the appropriate accounts on 1 September.

b Prepare the cash book and the ledgers by entering the transactions. Balance the cash book on 30 September and bring down the balances on 1 October 20–9.

c Transfer the totals of the discount columns in the cash book to the ledger.

d Prepare the accounts of the trade receivables and trade payables, totalling or balancing the accounts as required. [36]

5 On 1 March 20–9 the balance of the bank column in Min's cash book was $2 200 credit.

The transactions for the month of March 20–9 were:

March 3	Paid wages by cheque, $425.
6	Salema, a credit customer, paid her debt of $400 by credit transfer, after deducting a cash discount of 5%.
15	Paid a cheque to Harrison, a supplier, in full settlement of his account of $1 200, less 3% cash discount.
22	Received and banked a cheque from Lorna, a credit customer, $150.
25	Paid electricity, $135, by direct debit.
30	The bank returned the cheque received from Lorna on 22 March as dishonoured.
31	Received a bank loan of $6 000.

Prepare the bank and discount columns of the cash book for March 20–9. Balance the bank column and bring down the balance on 1 April 20–9. [8]

Revision checklist

In this chapter you have learnt:

- that the ledger is usually split into the sales ledger, the purchases ledger and the nominal ledger so that the job of posting accounting entries can be divided up, and for easier reference

- the importance of the cash book for cash, bank and cash discounts, and that it is both a ledger account and a book of prime entry

- that trade discounts are a way to negotiate payment and are not recorded in the accounting records, whereas cash discounts are to encourage swift payment and are included in the accounting records

- the different ways that payments can be made via the bank, such as direct debits, standing orders and credit transfers.

Petty cash books

Learning summary

By the end of this chapter you should understand:

- ☐ the use of, and be able to process, accounting data in the petty cash book
- ☐ how to apply the imprest system of petty cash.

> **TERMS**
>
> **Analysis columns** are used to divide the payments into different categories.
>
> The **imprest system** of petty cash is where the amount spent each period is restored so that the petty cashier starts each period with the same amount.
>
> The **petty cash book** is used to record low value cash payments.

The use of the petty cash book

The petty cash book is used to record low-value cash payments, such as postage, cleaning and travel expenses. It serves two purposes as it lists the transactions for transferring to ledger accounts and also acts as a ledger account for petty cash transactions. It is both a book of prime entry and a ledger account in the same way that the cash book is. Keeping a petty cash book helps to reduce the number of entries in the cash book and is a good task for a more junior member of staff to carry out. The basic idea of the system is that the main cashier will give the petty cashier an amount of cash sufficient to cover expenses for the day, week or month.

The document which acts as proof of the transaction for the petty cash book is called the petty cash voucher. This records the purpose for which the money is needed, the date and the signature of the person receiving the cash. Employees will need to provide proof of their expenditure, for example a receipt for petrol purchased. This can then be attached to the petty cash voucher. Each petty cash voucher has a number which is recorded in the petty cash book. In the sample answers below the voucher number has been abbreviated to 'Vo. no.' in the petty cash book.

The imprest system

A cash float is drawn from the bank and replenished as necessary, often weekly. Each time, the amount added back into petty cash will make up the expenditure and return the float back to the original amount. This is known as the imprest system. For example, if a business has spent $33 on petty cash items in a week then the cashier will need to receive $33 to cover this expenditure. The amount of the imprest can be adjusted as needed in order to reflect the needs of the business. For example, if the business increased the number of employees then the number of petty cash claims is likely to increase and so the imprest will need to increase too.

It is very unlikely, but possible, to have other types of receipts in the petty cash book other than the cash introduced to top up the imprest. For example, a small refund due to being overcharged by the window cleaner. In this case, the income is listed under the balance b/d and is added onto the cash. We will effectively have less to top up at the end of the week or month due to the additional income.

Sample questions

1 Which transaction would not belong in the petty cash book?

A payment for coffee

B payment for loan interest

C payment for petrol

D payment for postage

Answer: B would belong in the cash book, in the bank column, and not in the petty cash book. The petty cash book is for low value items using cash.

2 Edith keeps a petty cash book using the imprest system. Her imprest is $200. The following transactions have taken place during the first week of June:

20–8		$	Voucher number
June 1	Balance	200	
1	Travel expenses	30	18
2	Employee's bed and breakfast	38	19
3	Travel expenses	24	20
5	Stamps	25	21
5	Cleaning materials	21	22
6	Employee's bed and breakfast	38	23

a Prepare Edith's petty cash book for the first week of June 20–8. The petty cash book should have four analysis columns – travel, accommodation, postage and cleaning.

b Balance the petty cash book on 7 June and carry down the balance. Show the restoration of the imprest on 8 June 20–8.

c Make the necessary entries in Edith's nominal ledger on 7 June 20–8.

Answer:

Edith
Petty cash book

Date	Details	Total received $	Date	Details	Vo. no.	Total paid $	Travel $	Accom. $	Postage $	Cleaning $
20–8			20–8							
June 1	Bal b/d	200	June 1	Travel expenses	18	30	30			
			2	B&B	19	38		38		
			3	Travel expenses	20	24	24			
			5	Stamps	21	25			25	
			5	Cleaning materials	22	21				21
			6	B&B	23	38		38		
						176	54	76	25	21
			7	Bal c/d		24	nl 5	nl 8	nl 22	nl 23
		200				200				
20–8										
June 8	Bal b/d	24								
	Cash	176								

Edith
Nominal ledger
Travel account page 5

Date	Details	$	Date	Details	$
20–8					
June 7	Petty cash	54			

Accommodation account page 8

Date	Details	$	Date	Details	$
20–8					
June 7	Petty cash	76			

Postage account page 22

Date	Details	$	Date	Details	$
20–8					
June 7	Petty cash	25			

Cleaning account page 23

Date	Details	$	Date	Details	$
20–8					
June 7	Petty cash	21			

> **TIP**
> Sometimes a business may choose to pay a trade payable using petty cash and this is demonstrated in the following question. If a business does not have a particular column for an expense then it can be placed in the sundry or miscellaneous column. In the question below we will use the sundry expenses column for items which are not travel or cleaning expenses.

3 Fabio keeps a petty cash book using the imprest system. His imprest is $250. The following transactions have taken place during the month of March 20–9:

20–9		$	Voucher number
Mar 1	Balance	250	
1	Travel expenses	36	12
14	Paid L Binyon, a credit supplier	20	13
16	Petrol expenses	24	14
22	Coffee	3	15
25	Cleaning materials	12	16
29	Window cleaner	8	17

a Prepare Fabio's petty cash book for the month of March 20–9. The petty cash book should have four analysis columns – travel, cleaning, sundry expenses and ledger accounts.

b Balance the petty cash book on 31 March 20–9 and carry down the balance. Show the restoration of the imprest on 1 April 20–9.

c Make the necessary entries in Fabio's nominal ledger and purchases ledger on 31 March 20–9.

Answer:

Fabio
Petty cash book

Date	Details	Total Received $	Date	Details	Vo. no.	Total paid $	Travel $	Cleaning $	Sundry $	Ledger $
20–9			20–9							
Mar 1	Bal b/d	250	Mar 1	Travel expenses	12	36	36			
30	Refund from window cleaner	2	14	L Binyon	13	20				20
			16	Petrol	14	24	24			
			22	Coffee	15	3			3	
			25	Cleaning materials	16	12		12		
			29	Window cleaner	17	8		8		
						103	60	20	3	20
				Bal c/d	7	149	nl 2	nl 11	nl 20	
		252				252				
20–9										
Apr 1	Bal b/d	149								
	Cash	101								

Due to the receipt from the window cleaner, it is only necessary for the imprest to be $101 rather than the $103 which was recorded as being spent.

Fabio
Nominal ledger
Travel account page 2

Date	Details	$	Date	Details	$
20–9					
Mar 31	Petty cash	60			

Cleaning account page 11

Date	Details	$	Date	Details	$
20–9			20–9		
Mar 31	Petty cash	20	Mar 31	Petty cash	2

Sundry expenses account page 20

Date	Details	$	Date	Details	$
20–9					
Mar 31	Petty cash	3			

Purchases ledger
L Binyon account

Date	Details	$	Date	Details	$
20–9					
Mar 14	Petty cash	20			

> **TIPS**
>
> Always add across the totals of the analysis columns to check that they match the total of all transactions.
>
> Most businesses have a column for small value items which do not fit into the other analysis columns. This is sometimes called sundry expenses or miscellaneous items. If you are struggling to know where to place an item this is often the column where the item belongs.

Progress check

1 What type of financial transactions are recorded in the petty cash book?
2 Explain the imprest system.
3 Give three examples of analysis columns that a business may use.

Examination-style questions

1. Atiqa keeps an analysed petty cash book. The cash float at the start of each month is $150 and the imprest system is maintained at the end of the month.

20–8		$	Voucher number
Apr 1	Balance	150	
2	Envelopes	5	43
5	Bus fares	8	44
10	Window cleaner	7	45
12	Photocopying	12	46
18	Rail ticket	23	47
21	Printer cartridge	34	48
23	Petrol	16	49
25	Bus fares	2	50
29	Cleaning cloths	7	51
30	Petrol	22	52

   Prepare Atiqa's petty cash book for the month of April 20–8. The petty cash book should have three analysis columns – travel, stationery and cleaning. Balance the cash book on 30 April 20–8 and carry down the balance. Give the restoration of the imprest on 1 May 20–8. [15]

2. On returning from holiday, you are told to take over the petty cash book by your manager. This is kept on the imprest system, the float being $125 at the beginning of each month. Analysis columns are used for travel, postage, stationery and meals.

20–8		$	Voucher number
Aug 1	Balance	125	
3	Taxi fare	5	33
6	Parcel postage	2	34
7	Pencils	1	35
9	Train fare	5	36
12	Lunch with client	12	37
14	Large envelopes	2	38
16	Petrol	10	39
19	Meal allowance	5	40
20	Recorded delivery postage	2	41
23	Roll of packing tape	1	42
25	Excess postage paid	3	43
28	Taxi fare	6	44

   Prepare the petty cash book for the month of August 20–8. Balance the book at 31 August 20–8 and restore the imprest on 1 September 20–8. Make the necessary entries in the nominal ledger. [21]

3 Marina keeps an analysed petty cash book using the imprest system. The amount of the imprest is $200. She provided the following information:

20–7		$	Voucher number
Feb 2	Pencils	4	30
5	Bus fares	8	31
10	Flowers	5	32
12	Paper	12	33
18	Rail ticket	35	34
21	Printer cartridge	42	35
23	Petrol	16	36
25	Bus fares	4	37
26	Cleaning materials	7	38
27	Refund on damaged printer cartridge	6	
28	Petrol	19	39

Prepare Marina's petty cash book for the month of February 20–7. The petty cash book should have four analysis columns – travel, motor, stationery and sundry expenses. Balance the petty cash book on 28 February and carry down the balance. Give the restoration of the imprest on 1 March 20–7. [20]

4 On 1 July the petty cash balance equalled the imprest amount of $250. During July the petty cashier spent $95 and received a refund for cleaning materials of $12.

What entry will be made on 31 July to restore the imprest? [1]

	Debit	$	Credit	$
A	Bank	83	Petty cash book	83
B	Bank	95	Petty cash book	95
C	Petty cash book	83	Bank	83
D	Petty cash book	95	Bank	95

5 Where are the balances in the petty cash book transferred to at the end of the period? [4]

Revision checklist

In this chapter you have learnt:

- that the petty cash book is used for low value cash payments and it is both a book of prime entry and a ledger account, like the cash book

- how to apply the imprest system of petty cash which involves topping up the petty cash account, either weekly or monthly, with the same amount which has been spent.

Section 2

Chapter 6

Business documents

Learning summary

By the end of this chapter you should understand:

- and recognise the following business documents: invoice, debit note, credit note, statement of account, cheque and receipt
- how to complete proforma business documents
- the use of business documents as sources of information
- how to account for trade discount.

TERMS

A **cheque** is a written order to a bank to pay a stated sum of money to the person or business named on the order.

A **credit note** is a document issued by a seller of goods on credit to notify of a reduction in an invoice previously issued.

A **debit note** is a document issued by a purchaser of goods on credit to request a reduction in the invoice received.

An **invoice** is a document issued by the supplier of goods on credit showing details, quantities and prices of goods supplied.

A **receipt** is a written acknowledgement of money received and acts as proof of payment.

A **statement of account** is a document issued by the seller of goods on credit to summarise the transactions for the month.

Purpose of business documents

Financial transactions involve a range of business documents, each of which needs to be accurately completed and recorded. The use of written documents allows both buyer and seller to have a clear understanding of the trading arrangements. They confirm each stage of the transaction: the buyer's requirements; the prices to be paid to the seller; the delivery of the goods or services; the amount owed by the buyer; the time within which payment must be paid; and, finally, the amount paid. Documents also constitute legally binding evidence in cases of dispute. Think of business documents as the proof of a transaction taking place.

Invoice

When a business provides goods on credit it will need to issue an invoice. As far as the supplier is concerned this document is a sales invoice. However, from the customer's viewpoint it is an incoming purchase invoice, detailing what has been bought and how much is due to the supplier. In other words, the same document serves two purposes depending on which side of the transaction you are, buyer or seller.

The invoice shows details about the supplier, the customer, the date of sale, the details of goods or services supplied and the terms of trade. There may be a trade discount given to encourage repeat buying or buying in bulk. This is shown as a deduction on the invoice but is not recorded in the accounting records. Cash discount, however, is not shown as a deduction on the invoice and is a reward to the customer for paying by a certain date. This type of discount is recorded in the accounting records, and eventually in the financial statements, as discount received or discount allowed.

Sample question

1

Sizzlers Catering Services
Unit 4a
New Business Park
Shoreham-by-Sea
SH14 6UT

Tel: 01856 342697

Invoice 112

15 August 20–9

Invoice to:
The Grand Hotel
The Promenade
Shoreham-by-Sea
SH23 8AH

Product	Quantity	Unit price $	Amount $
Microwave oven MO17654	1	120.45	
Pasta cookers BM 453H	3	46.20	
Serviette holders SSC 4528	80	1.40	
Water coolers VP 7658	4	18.20	

Terms: 3% cash discount if account paid by 31 August 20–9

Less 10% trade discount

Amount payable

Calculate the missing figures in the above invoice and calculate how much will be paid if the cash discount is received.

Answer: The total of the goods before the trade discount is $443.85 and the trade discount is $44.39, leaving the amount payable as $399.46. If this is paid by 31 August 20–9 then the cash discount will be $11.98 leaving $387.48 to pay.

Debit note

If it is discovered that a delivery of goods has any shortages, overcharges or faults then the business receiving the goods can let the supplier know this using a debit note. The debit note contains the names and addresses of both customer and supplier, the date and full details and quantities of goods returned or overcharged. It is important to remember that a debit note is not recorded in either the accounting records of the customer or the supplier and is just a mechanism to ask for the original invoice amount to be reduced.

Credit note

Sometimes not all the goods that are ordered arrive in good condition. They may have been damaged or lost in transit, incorrect items or quantities may have been sent or they may be faulty. When this occurs, the supplier sends the customer a credit note. A credit note is very similar to an invoice but, instead of increasing the customer's debt to the supplier, a credit note reduces the debt. In other words, it is the opposite of an invoice for accounting purposes. Credit notes detail very similar information to invoices, usually with the addition of an explanation of why the credit is being issued. Unlike debit notes, the customer records the credit note in purchases returns and the supplier in sales returns.

Sample question

2

Sizzlers Catering Services
Unit 4a
New Business Park
Shoreham-by-Sea
SH14 6UT

Tel: 01856 342697

Credit note C 98

20 August 20–9

Credit note to:
The Grand Hotel
The Promenade
Shoreham-by-Sea
SH23 8AH

Product	Quantity	Unit price $	Amount $
Water coolers VP 7658	4	18.20	
Less 10% trade discount			
Reason for issue of credit note:			
Damaged goods			

Calculate the missing figures in the above credit note.

Answer: $72.80 – trade discount of $7.28 = $65.52

Statement of account

It is essential to remind customers at the end of each month how much they owe you to ensure effective credit control. The statement of account lists all the invoices and credit notes that have been sent to the customer during the month, together with any payments that have been received from the customer. The total of the statement, therefore, is the outstanding amount currently due to be paid by the customer.

Sample question

3

Sizzlers Catering Services
Unit 4a
New Business Park
Shoreham-by-Sea
SH14 6UT

Tel: 01856 342697

Statement of account

31 August 20–9

Invoice to:
The Grand Hotel
The Promenade
Shoreham-by-Sea
SH23 8AH

Date	Reference	Debit $	Credit $	Balance $
20–9 August 15	Invoice number 112	399.46		
August 20	Credit note C98		65.52	

Terms: 3% cash discount if account paid by 31 August 20–9

Calculate the balance figures for 15 and 20 August.

Answer: The balance figure for 15 August is $399.46 and the balance figure for 20 August is $333.94. This reminds the customer of the balance owing for the month of August and it takes account of the goods which were returned.

Cheque

Increasingly, businesses are choosing to use credit transfers to settle debts owed but some may still prefer to use cheques. A cheque is a written order to a bank to pay a stated sum of money to the person or business named on the order. The person writing out the cheque is known as the drawer and person to whom it is payable is known as the payee. Cheques must be written clearly, in ink, with the amount written in both words and figures. The name of the payee must appear and the cheque must be dated and signed by the drawer.

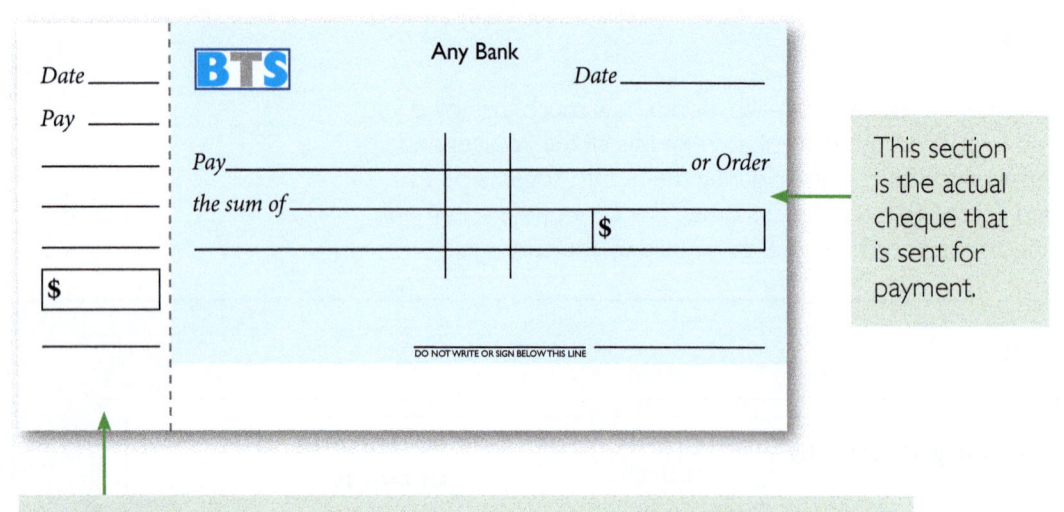

This section is the actual cheque that is sent for payment.

This section is known as the counterfoil; this part is kept by the issuer. Each time a cheque is written and sent the details of:

- who it was sent to
- when it was sent
- and for how much money

are recorded. This is then used by the business as a source document to record in the cash book how much money went out via cheque payments.

Receipt

Every time you go to a shop and buy something, paying immediately, using cash or paying with a debit or credit card, you will be given a receipt. This receipt is proof of your purchase and is kept by the business to enter into its accounts as a record of money spent.

> **TIPS**
>
> Think of the business documents as the evidence or proof of the transaction taking place.
>
> You need to remember whose point of view you are considering the business document from, the seller or the buyer.
>
> Remember that trade discounts are not included in the accounting records but cash discounts are.

Progress check

1. What is the difference between a debit note and a credit note?
2. What is the purpose of a statement of account?
3. What is the similarity between an invoice and a receipt?

Examination-style questions

1. a Give the name of the document that was issued by Marija to Nikola for the following dates: [2]
      i   12 July   Nikola purchased goods on credit from Marija.
      ii 14 July   Nikola returned to Marija some of the goods purchased on 12 July.
   b Give the name of the document that Marija may issue to Nikola on 30 July. [1]

2. Prepare the following table using the source document and relevant double entry for the accounting records of Suranne. The first one has been completed as an example. [9]

Transaction	Source document	Account to debit	Account to credit
Suranne bought goods on credit from Solo Ltd	Purchase invoice	Purchases	Solo Ltd
Suranne sold goods on credit to Rayner			
Rayner returned some faulty goods to Suranne			
Suranne bought goods for cash			

3.

Seasons greetings   **Invoice 468**
Unit 4a   Tel: 01856 342698
New Business Park
Shoreham-by-Sea
SH14 6UT

                                 12 April 20–9

Invoice to:
News Are Us
The Precinct
Shoreham-by-Sea
SH23 8AH

Product	Quantity	Unit price $	Amount $
Greeting cards various	150	0.60	?
Wrapping paper metallic	44	2.25	?
Gift tags – pack of 10	60	1.10	?
Glitter spray	80	3.10	?
			?
Terms: 5% cash discount if account paid by 30 April 20–9		Less 15% trade discount	?
		Amount payable	?

Calculate the missing figures and then calculate how much will be paid if the cash discount is received. [8]

4 A credit customer buys goods with a list price of $3 000. Trade discount is 25% and cash discount is 6%.
   Which amount is entered in the customer's account to record the sale? [1]

   A $2 070   B $2 115   C $2 250   D $2 820

5 Name the following business documents. [4]

Document
A demand for payment
A written acknowledgement of money received
A summary of transactions for a period issued to a customer
Issued by a purchaser of goods on credit to request a reduction in the invoice received

Revision checklist

In this chapter you have learnt:

- ☐ to recognise the following business documents, how to complete them and how they are sources of information:

  - invoice – could be a sales invoice (if the business is selling goods on credit) or a purchase invoice (if the business is buying goods on credit)
  - debit note – alerts a business that you are returning goods and the reason why
  - credit note – issued to a business returning goods to state a reduction in the sales invoice total
  - statement of account – acts as a reminder of transactions during the month between the buyer and seller
  - cheque – payment method using the bank account
  - receipt – proof of purchase when paying for goods or services immediately.

Books of prime entry

Chapter 7

Learning summary

By the end of this chapter you should understand:

- the advantage of using various books of prime entry
- the use of, and be able to process, accounting data in the books of prime entry – sales journal, purchases journal, sales returns journal and purchases returns journal
- how to post the ledger entries from the books of prime entry.

TERMS

A book of prime entry is one in which transactions are recorded before being entered in the ledger.

The purchases journal shows a list of the names of businesses from which credit purchases have been made, the value of the goods purchased and the date on which the purchases were made.

The purchases returns journal shows a list of the names of businesses to which goods, previously purchased on credit, have been returned, the value of the goods returned and the date on which the returns were made.

The sales journal shows a list of the names of businesses to which credit sales have been made, the value of the goods sold and the date on which the sales were made.

The sales returns journal shows a list of the names of the businesses which have returned goods previously sold on credit, the value of the goods returned and the date on which the returns were made.

Advantages of using books of prime entry

The books of prime entry are the:

- cash book = any transaction involving the bank or cash
- petty cash book = low value items in cash
- sales journal = selling goods on credit, sales invoice issued
- purchases journal = buying goods on credit, purchase invoice received
- sales returns journal = returned items previously sold, credit note issued
- purchases returns journal = returning items to supplier, credit note received.

The books are used to list and group together similar transactions which means that totals can then be posted to the ledger. This allows the work to be divided between different members of staff. Some large businesses may have a purchase ledger clerk and all they are concerned with is recording transactions in the purchases journal. The totals from the books of prime entry can be used for control accounts (Chapter 16).

Sales journal

The evidence used to prepare the sales journal is from copies of sales invoices which have been issued to the credit customers.

When goods are sold on credit	At the end of the month
Record the date, customer name and invoice total in the sales journal.	Credit the sales account in the nominal ledger with the sales journal total.
Debit the customer's account in the sales ledger with the same amount.	This will now form the double entry for all the individual debit entries in the sales ledger.

Sales returns journal

Sometimes customers will wish to return goods they have purchased because they have over ordered, or the goods are faulty, for example. In this case the transaction is recorded in the sales returns journal and the customer is issued with a credit note.

When goods are returned by a credit customer	At the end of the month
Record the date, customer name and credit note total in the sales returns journal.	Debit the sales returns account in the nominal ledger with the sales returns journal total.
Credit the customer's account in the sales ledger with the same amount.	This will now form the double entry for all the individual credit entries in the sales ledger.

TIPS

Remember, trade discount is not recorded in the double entry records but cash discount is.

List price is the amount before trade discount has been removed, so if sales had a trade discount to be applied then this needs to be reflected in the amount of the sales returns too.

It is important to state if a credit note has been received or issued as it is the same business document for both sales returns and purchases returns.

Sample question

1

20–9		
Mar 4	Sizzlers issued an invoice to the Grand Hotel for goods, $620, and allowed a trade discount of 20%
9	Sizzlers issued a credit note to the Grand Hotel for goods returned, list price $100
15	Sizzlers sent HCC an invoice for $350 for goods supplied on credit
18	Sizzlers issued a credit note to HCC for $15 because of an overcharge

Prepare the necessary entries in the books of Sizzlers for March 20–9.

Answer:

Sizzlers
Sales journal

Date	Name	Invoice number	Amount $
20–9			
Mar 4	Grand Hotel	1120	496
15	HCC	1121	350
31	Transfer to sales account		846

Sales returns journal

Date	Name	Credit note number	Amount $
20–9			
Mar 9	Grand Hotel	C 36	80
18	HCC	C 37	15
31	Transfer to sales returns account		95

Sales ledger
Grand Hotel account

Date	Details	$	Date	Details	$
20–9			20–9		
Mar 4	Sales	496	Mar 9	Sales returns	80

HCC account

Date	Details	$	Date	Details	$
20–9			20–9		
Mar 15	Sales	350	Mar 18	Sales returns	15

Nominal ledger
Sales account

Date	Details	$	Date	Details	$
			20–9		
			Mar 31	Credit sales for month	846

Sales returns account

Date	Details	$	Date	Details	$
20–9					
Mar 31	Returns for month	95			

Purchases journal

The evidence used to prepare the purchases journal is from purchase invoices which have been received from credit suppliers. If a business pays straight away for goods then the transaction is recorded in the cash book and the business document is a receipt.

When goods are purchased on credit	At the end of the month
Record the date, supplier name and invoice total in the purchases journal.	Debit the purchases account in the nominal ledger with the purchases journal total.
Credit the supplier's account in the purchases ledger with the same amount.	This will now form the double entry for all the individual credit entries in the purchases ledger.

Purchases returns journal

The purchases returns journal is for the business to record any goods it has returned itself for the same reasons as sales returns may occur. Again, the evidence is the credit note, but in this case the credit note received.

When goods are returned to a credit supplier	At the end of the month
Record the date, supplier name and credit note total in the purchases returns journal.	Credit the purchases returns account in the nominal ledger with the purchases returns journal total.
Debit the supplier's account in the purchases ledger with the same amount.	This will now form the double entry for all the individual debit entries in the purchases ledger.

Sample question

2

20–9	
Mar 4	The Grand Hotel received a purchase invoice for goods purchased from Sizzlers for $620 and allowed a trade discount of 20%
9	The Grand Hotel received a credit note from Sizzlers for goods returned, list price $100
21	The Grand Hotel received an invoice for goods purchased on credit from Cool Drinks for $450
24	The Grand Hotel discovered a faulty batch of drinks and returned them to Cool Drinks who issued a credit note for $25

Prepare the necessary entries in the books of the Grand Hotel for March 20–9.

Answer:

The Grand Hotel
Purchases journal

Date	Name	Invoice number	Amount $
20–9			
Mar 4	Sizzlers	1120	496
21	Cool Drinks	12128	450
31	Transfer to purchases account		946

Purchases returns journal

Date	Name	Credit note number	Amount $
20–9			
Mar 9	Sizzlers	C 36	80
24	Cool Drinks	C 489	25
31	Transfer to purchases returns account		105

Purchases ledger
Sizzlers account

Date	Details	$	Date	Details	$
20–9			20–9		
Mar 9	Purchases returns	80	Mar 4	Purchases	496

Cool Drinks account

Date	Details	$	Date	Details	$
20–9			20–9		
Mar 24	Purchases returns	25	Mar 21	Purchases	450

Nominal ledger
Purchases account

Date	Details	$	Date	Details	$
20–9					
Mar 31	Credit purchases for month	946			

Purchases returns account

Date	Details	$	Date	Details	$
			20–9		
			Mar 31	Returns for month	105

Progress check

1 Name four books of prime entry.
2 What is the purpose of a sales journal?
3 Give two reasons why goods may be returned.
4 Where are the totals for the sales journal and purchases journal posted to?

Examination-style questions

1 Prepare the following table giving the book of prime entry for each of the source documents. The first has been completed as an example. [4]

Source document	Book of prime entry
Cheque counterfoil	*Cash book*
Sales invoice	
Credit note received	
Purchase invoice	
Credit note issued	

2   Prepare the following table for **each** of Lorenzo's transactions in June 20–9. The first transaction has been completed as an example. [12]

Transaction	Book of prime entry	Account to be debited	Account to be credited
Bought goods on credit from Maurizio	*Purchases journal*	*Purchases*	*Maurizio*
Paolo returned goods			
Paid rent by standing order			
Sold goods to Roman for cash			
Sold goods to Becca on credit			

3   Cassie provided the following information about Sid, one of her credit suppliers:

20–8		
Apr 1	Cassie owed $560	
3	Cassie purchased goods, list price $840, less 20% trade discount	
6	Cassie returned goods, list price $150, purchased on 3 April	
18	Cassie purchased goods, list price $320, no trade discount	
29	Cassie paid the balance of her account on 1 April by bank transfer and deducted 5% cash discount	

Prepare the account of Sid in the ledger of Cassie. Balance the account and bring down the balance on 1 May 20–8. [6]

4   Quaid is a trader. His transactions in October 20–9 included the following:

20–9	
Oct 1	Purchased goods from Kate for $2 200, less 20% trade discount
4	Sold goods to Emily for $4 600, less 15% trade discount
8	Returned goods to Kate purchased on 1 October, list price $40
13	Purchased goods from Sienna for $1 300
15	Emily returned goods purchased on 4 October, list price $1 200
16	Sold goods to Emily for $3 400, less 15% trade discount
28	Returned goods to Sienna at list price, $75

a   Prepare the journals by entering these transactions in Quaid's sales, purchases and returns journals for October 20–9.

b   Prepare the following accounts in Quaid's ledger for October 20–9:

sales, purchases, sales returns, purchases returns, Kate, Emily and Sienna. It is not necessary to balance or total any of the accounts. [18]

5   Which book of prime entry is used to record cash sales? [1]

A   Cash book   C   Sales returns journal
B   Sales journal   D   Purchases journal

Revision checklist

In this chapter you have learnt:

- the advantage of using various books of prime entry so that similar transactions can be listed together and allow different members of staff to share work (there is no double entry at this stage)
- the sales journal is for recording credit sales and the business document is the sales invoice
- the purchases journal is for recording credit purchases and the business document is the purchases invoice
- the sales returns journal is for recording returns by credit customers and the business document is the credit note issued
- the purchases returns journal is for goods returned to credit suppliers and the business document is the credit note received
- at the end of each month the totals of the books of prime entry are posted to the relevant accounts and this is where double entry occurs.

Section 3

Chapter 8

Financial statements – Part A

Learning summary

By the end of this chapter you should understand:

- ■ the advantages and disadvantages of operating as a sole trader
- ■ the importance of preparing income statements
- ■ the difference between a trading business and a service business
- ■ how to prepare income statements for trading businesses and service businesses
- ■ how to make adjustments for goods taken by the owner for own use
- ■ how to balance ledger accounts and make transfers to financial statements.

TERMS

The *income statement* is a statement prepared for a trading period to show the gross profit and profit for the year.

A *service business* is one which provides a service.

A *sole trader* is a business owned by one individual. They may employ others so do not necessarily work alone.

A *trading business* is one which buys and sells goods.

Advantages and disadvantages of operating a sole trader

A common misconception is that a sole trader just works on their own. This is not true; what it means is that the ownership of the business is by just one person. A sole trader can employ staff so you should not assume that they have no employees. Setting up as a sole trader is very easy and does not require an accountant or legal assistance.

Advantages include:

- Independence – you can make your own decisions and not rely on partners or shareholders who may not always agree with you. You can also decide on your own working hours, although many sole traders often work far more hours than if they were employed by someone else, but it does provide flexibility.
- Profit – any profit made is kept by the sole trader and does not have to be shared.

Disadvantages include:

- Unlimited liability – you are taking a risk that if the business does not succeed then you will solely be liable for all the debts of the business. This means your own personal assets, such as house and car, could be sold in order to cover the amount owing.

- Lack of capital – if it is just you on your own then your finance could be limited in terms of what you can put into the business initially. It can also be harder to raise finance from financial institutions such as banks as you are seen as a higher risk on your own.

Importance of preparing income statements

An income statement contains revenues and expenses for a specific period. It provides key information which helps the business to make decisions in terms of finding new suppliers in order to cut cost of sales, or increasing prices to increase gross profit and profit for the year.

An income statement is split into two sections. The trading section is where the gross profit is calculated and the profit and loss section is where the profit for the year is calculated.

The difference between an income statement for a trading business and a service business

A trading business buys and sells goods and will make use of the trading section of the income statement where the cost of sales is subtracted from revenue to find gross profit. A service business, for example a property rental agency, will not have use for this section and will start the profit and loss section with the rental income gained rather than the gross profit. Both types of business will then subtract expenses in order to calculate the profit or loss for the year. This crucial figure also then appears in the statement of financial position which is examined in Chapter 9.

How to prepare the trading section of the income statement

Omari
Income statement (trading section) for the year ended 31 July 20–8

	$	$
Revenue		452 000
Less Sales returns	20 000	432 000
Less Cost of sales		
Opening inventory	50 000	
Purchases	300 000	
Less Purchases returns	10 000	
Less Goods for own use	1 000	
Carriage inwards	2 000	
Less Closing inventory	35 000	
		306 000
Gross profit		126 000

'Sales' is now called 'revenue' when the financial statements are prepared. The cost of sales figure of $306 000 is calculated by starting with the opening inventory (the inventory the business owns at the start of the year) and then adjusting until finally the closing inventory (the inventory owned at the end of the financial year) is subtracted. The reason for subtracting the closing inventory is that this will be sold the following financial year, so this becomes the new opening inventory. It is the closing inventory which will go into the current assets section of the statement of financial position. Note the goods for own use; these are drawings which the owner has made so need adding onto drawings on the statement of financial position. Carriage inwards is the delivery charge for goods which we purchase so needs adding to purchases as it makes our goods more expensive. Carriage outwards is when we pay for delivery on behalf of our customers so this goes into expenses.

How to prepare the profit and loss section of the income statement

Omari
Income statement (profit and loss section) for the year ended 31 July 20–8

	$	$
Gross profit		306 000
Add Discount received		2 000	308 000
Less Expenses		
Discount allowed	2 200	
Wages	17 500	
Light and heat	3 330	
Carriage outwards	850	23 880
Profit from operations		284 120
Less Loan interest		1 500
Profit for the year		282 620

The profit and loss section adds any other type of income which is not from sales and then all expenses are subtracted. Loan interest has its own section and is subtracted from profit from operations to finally produce the profit for the year. If you calculate a negative figure you must label it as loss for the year.

If the business is a service business, then simply replace the gross profit with whatever the business receives instead of the revenue from selling goods. For example, a property rental agent would receive rent from its tenants and an accountant would receive fees from their clients.

Transferring ledger account totals to the income statement

When an income statement is prepared the information is usually taken from the trial balance. The figures from the trial balance come from the ledger accounts which need to be balanced in order to establish the amounts up to the end of that period.

Items debited to the income statement, such as expenses, will need to be credited in the appropriate ledger account. Items credited to the income statement, such as sales, will need to be debited in the ledger account.

Omari
Nominal ledger
Wages account

Date	Details	$	Date	Details	$
20–8			20–8		
July 31	Total to date	17 500	July 31	Income statement	17 500
		17 500			17 500

Sales account

Date	Details	$	Date	Details	$
20–8			20–8		
July 31	Income statement	452 000	July 31	Total to date	452 000
		452 000			452 000

Progress check

1 What is the difference between a service business and a trading business?
2 Define an income statement.
3 Where do items for the income statement originate from?

Sample questions

1 The following balances were extracted from the books of Harvest Moon Designs at 31 December 20–8:

	$
Carriage outwards	450
Purchases	15 467
Property tax	1 300
Sales returns	659
Purchases returns	321
Revenue	62 579
Inventory at 1 December	5 502
Inventory at 31 December	4 892
General expenses	2 500
Wages	12 200
Loan interest	1 200

Prepare the income statement for the year ended 31 December 20–8.

Answer:

Harvest Moon Designs
Income statement for the year ended 31 December 20–8

	$	$
Revenue	62 579	
Less Sales returns	659	61 920
Less Cost of sales		
Opening inventory	5 502	
Purchases	15 467	
Less Purchases returns	321	
Less Closing inventory	4 892	15 756
Gross profit		46 164
Less Expenses		
Property tax	1 300	
Wages	12 200	
General expenses	2 500	16 000
Profit from operations		30 164
Less Loan interest		1 200
Profit for the year		28 964

2 Surina is a children's entertainer and she has extracted a trial balance at 31 March 20–8. She would now like you to prepare her income statement for the year ended 31 March 20–8.

	Dr $	Cr $
Fees received		100 326
Wages and salaries	42 255	
Property tax	5 000	
Heating and lighting	2 487	
Postage, telephone and stationery	1 399	
Advertising	8 660	
General expenses	7 600	
Motor vehicle	20 000	
Receivables	2 130	
Bank	8 412	
Cash	498	
Owner's equity		52 000
Drawings	53 885	
	152 326	152 326

Answer: There are items in the trial balance which will not go into the income statement because they belong on the statement of financial position. These are assets, liabilities or owner's equity. This income statement does not require a trading account as Surina does not buy and sell goods; she provides a service.

Fees received		100 326
Less Expenses		
Property tax	5 000	
Wages and salaries	42 255	
Heating and lighting	2 487	
Advertising	8 660	
General expenses	7 600	66 002
Profit for the year		34 324

There is no loan interest for this answer as Surina does not have a loan.

TIPS

It is a good idea to tick off items as you use them in the income statement. The items you are left with then belong on the statement of financial position.

The profit or loss from your income statement then goes onto the statement of financial position.

If a business has only just started trading that financial year, there will be no opening inventory.

Make sure you check if the business is a trading or service business before you start writing out the layout for the income statement.

Examination-style questions

1 Which group contains only service businesses? [1]

   A costume repair business, theatre bar, employment agency

   B dancing school, employment agency, costume repair business

   C dancing school, employment agency, dance wear shop

   D dance wear shop, costume repair business, theatre bar

2 Prepare the following table by using a tick to show whether each item can appear in the financial statements of a trading business, a service business, or both. [4]

	Trading business only	Service business only	Both
Opening inventory			
Gross profit			
Loan interest			
Loss for the year			

3. The owner of The Blooming Wildly Garden Centre needs to prepare the trading section of the income statement from the following information:

	$
Carriage inwards	3 400
Carriage outwards	2 974
Purchases	342 400
Sales returns	6 953
Purchases returns	2 560
Revenue	512 830
Inventory at 1 April 20–8	25 630
Inventory at 31 March 20–9	21 568

Prepare the trading section of the income statement for the year ended 31 March 20–9. [10]

4. The following balances are taken from the books of George showing totals for the year ended 31 December 20–8:

	$
Revenue	76 945
Purchases	43 982
Sales returns	2 900
Purchases returns	1 400
Carriage inwards	852
Carriage outwards	984
Inventory at 1 January 20–8	5 870
Inventory at 31 December 20–8	6 485
Wages	13 055
Property tax	1 600
Loan interest	950

Prepare the income statement for the year ended 31 December 20–8. [16]

5. The books of prime entry of Ashlin Trading show the following totals for the month of December 20–8:

Totals for the month	Total $
Sales day journal	6 847
Sales returns journal	278
Purchases journal	4 524
Purchases returns journal	149

Insert the above totals into the following ledger accounts and make transfers to the income statement.

Sales account

Date	Details	$	Date	Details	$
			20–8		
			Dec 1	Bal b/d	16 593

Sales returns account

Date	Details	$	Date	Details	$
20–8					
Dec 1	Bal b/d	1 279			

Purchases account

Date	Details	$	Date	Details	$
20–8					
Dec 1	Bal b/d	10 349			

Purchases returns account

Date	Details	$	Date	Details	$
			20–8		
			Dec 1	Bal b/d	1 049

The following information is also given:

	$
Inventory at 1 December 20–8	2 650
Inventory at 31 December 20–8	2 478
Carriage inwards for the month of December	782

Prepare the trading account section of the income statement for Ashlin Trading for the month ended 31 December 20–8. [18]

Revision checklist

In this chapter you have learnt:

- the advantages and disadvantages of operating as a sole trader
- the importance of preparing income statements in order to calculate gross profit and profit for the year
- the difference between a trading business and a service business – a service business does not buy and sell goods in the way a trading business does
- how to prepare income statements for trading businesses and service businesses, which is the same after gross profit
- how to make adjustments for goods taken by the owner for own use – these are known as drawings and need to appear in the cost of sales section on the income statement and in the capital section of the statement of financial position
- how to balance ledger accounts and make transfers to the income statement.

Financial statements – Part B

Chapter 9

Learning summary

By the end of this chapter you should understand:

- the importance of preparing statements of financial position
- that statements of financial position record assets and liabilities on a specified date
- the content of a statement of financial position: non-current assets, intangible assets, current assets, current liabilities, non-current liabilities and capital
- the inter-relationship of items in a statement of financial position
- how to prepare statements of financial position for trading businesses and service businesses.

TERMS

Current assets are short-term assets whose amounts are constantly changing.

Current liabilities are amounts owed which are due for repayment within the next 12 months.

Goodwill is the amount by which the value of a business as a whole exceeds the value of the net assets (total assets – total liabilities).

Non-current assets are assets which are obtained for use, not for resale, which help the business earn revenue.

Non-current liabilities are amounts owed which are not due for repayment within the next 12 months.

A **statement of financial position** is a statement of the assets and liabilities of a business on a certain date.

Importance of preparing a statement of financial position

In addition to the important information gained from the income statement, such as gross profit and profit for the year, it is also important for a business to know what it owns, what it owes and how this has been funded. This is found on a statement of financial position which shows assets and liabilities and is prepared at a particular time. The statement is only correct for one day, it is prepared at the year end and the title is at that date rather than for the year ended. It tells us how healthy the business is in terms of non-current assets and current assets that it owns and then how much it has borrowed from outside the business in order to fund these assets. The capital section is a reflection of what the owner has invested and then gained in profit or taken in drawings, and this matches the total assets minus total liabilities.

The layout for a statement of financial position

Vincent
Statement of financial position at 31 July 20–8

	$
Assets	
Non-current assets	
Property	150 000
Fixtures and equipment	15 000
	165 000
Current assets	
Inventory	35 000
Trade receivables	40 500
Bank	1 750
Cash	450
	77 700
Total assets	242 700
Capital and liabilities	
Capital	
Opening balance	30 000
Plus Profit for the year	282 620
Less Drawings	82 420
	230 200
Non-current liabilities	
Loan	10 000
Current liabilities	
Trade payables	2 500
Total capital and liabilities	242 700

The inter-relationship of items in the statement of financial position

Non-current assets are normally listed with the most permanent asset first. This is often property as it is not changed as often as, motor vehicles, for example, which may well be changed every couple of years.

Current assets are listed according to their liquidity. The least liquid item is listed first, inventory, as there is a chance a business may never find a buyer for the inventory as it may go out of fashion. This is followed by trade receivables as these credit customers have to be chased up to pay and some may never pay which will result in an irrecoverable debt (see Chapter 13). Obviously the most liquid asset is cash itself which is always listed last in the current assets.

Sample questions

1. Bryonie is confused about where to place items from the trial balance into the financial statements. Explain to her the key differences between the income statement and the statement of financial position.

   Answer: The income statement shows the income and expenses for a particular time period whereas the statement of financial position shows the assets, liabilities and capital at a specified date. If the items are from the business receiving or spending money then they are placed on the income statement. Once you have completed the income statement the items left should belong to the assets, liabilities or capital section of the statement of financial position.

2. On 30 April 20–9 the following figures were extracted from the ledgers of Harvey's Repairs:

	$
Bank loan – repayable in five years	25 000
Bank overdraft	1 200
Property	103 000
Capital at 1 May 20–8	110 000
Trade payables	3 600
Trade receivables	4 800
Drawings	13 525
Profit for the year	11 275
Fixtures and equipment	12 500
Inventory at 30 April 20–9	7 450
Motor vehicle	9 800

   Prepare a statement of financial position at 30 April 20–9.

Answer:

Harvey's Repairs
Statement of financial position at 30 April 20–9

	$
Assets	
Non-current assets	
Property	103 000
Fixtures and equipment	12 500
Motor vehicle	9 800
	125 300
Current assets	
Inventory	7 450
Trade receivables	4 800
	12 250
Total assets	137 550
Capital and liabilities	
Capital	
Opening balance	110 000
Plus Profit for the year	11 275
Less Drawings	13 525
	107 750
Non-current liabilities	
Loan	25 000
Current liabilities	
Trade payables	3 600
Bank overdraft	1 200
	4 800
Total capital and liabilities	137 550

In this question there is a bank overdraft. Even though a business will often have an overdraft for longer than 12 months, it is counted as a current liability as the bank could ask for the overdraft to be repaid at short notice. If there was a loss for the year on the income statement you would subtract the amount rather than adding it.

3 The following statement of financial position was drawn up by an inexperienced business owner, Peri. Prepare a corrected statement of financial position and calculate the missing profit.

Peri's Hair Design
Statement of financial position for the year ended 31 July 20–9

	$
Assets	
Non-current liabilities	
Loan	26 800
Non-current assets	
Property	250 500
Fixtures and equipment	16 600
	267 100
Current liabilities	
Trade receivables	3 800
Bank overdraft	2 400
	6 200
Current assets	
Inventory	4 900
Trade payables	2 360
	7 260
Total assets	273 300
Capital and liabilities	
Capital	
Opening balance	180 100
Less Profit for the year	?
Plus Drawings	3 800

Answer:

	$
Assets	
Non-current assets	
Property	250 500
Fixtures and equipment	16 600
	267 100
Current assets	
Inventory	4 900
Trade receivables	3 800
	8 700
Total assets	275 800
Capital and liabilities	
Capital	
Opening balance	180 100
Plus Profit for the year	67 940
Less Drawings	3 800
	244 240
Non-current liabilities	
Loan	26 800
Current liabilities	
Trade payables	2 360
Bank overdraft	2 400
Total capital and liabilities	275 800

In the original statement of financial position the non-current liabilities were in the wrong position at the top. They should appear below the capital section. Trade receivables and trade payables had been mixed up. Trade receivables are a current asset as they are credit customers who owe the business money. Trade payables are a current liability as they are amounts the business owes to credit suppliers which need paying within 12 months. Another error was in the capital section, where Peri thought she needed to subtract the profit and add the drawings made. Profit increases the amount of capital invested by the owner in the business. Drawings could be in the form of inventory or cash which the owner takes from the business for their own use. This has the effect of reducing the capital. If an owner takes excessive drawings then they risk running out of inventory or money to run the business.

Progress check

1. Explain how a non-current liability differs from a current liability.
2. State one reason why a business owner prepares a statement of financial position.
3. What is the difference between a tangible non-current and intangible non-current asset?

TIPS

It is the closing inventory which is included in the current assets on the statement of financial position.

Always use your own profit or loss from your income statement even if it means the statement of financial position will not balance. It is important that you know that the profit or loss calculated on the income statement is the same figure which appears in the capital section of the statement of financial position.

Check the amount that your statement of financial position does not balance by and look for the amount in the information given as you may have just missed off a balance.

If your statement of financial position does not balance then move onto the next question and come back to it later.

Examination-style questions

1. A statement of financial position showed the following:

	$
Non-current assets	225 200
Non-current liabilities	32 000
Current assets	72 000
Current liabilities	83 500

What was the owner's equity? [1]

A 20 500

B 101 700

C 181 700

D 245 700

2. Give the name of the section of a statement of financial position in which trade receivables are recorded. [1]

3. Prepare the table to state the effect of each of the following transactions made by Bayani in April 20–8. Where there is no effect write 'no effect'. The first transaction has been completed as an example. [9]

Transaction	Assets $	Liabilities $	Capital $
Purchased a motor vehicle on credit for $5 500	+5 500	+5 500	no effect
Sold goods on credit for $900 (cost $500)			
Obtained a bank loan for $10 000			
Paid a trade payable, $300, by cheque			

4 Abdul is a trader. Using the following information taken from Abdul's books on 31 March 20–8:

   a prepare a trial balance at 31 March 20–8. [21]

   b prepare an income statement for the year ended 31 March 20–8 [17]

   c prepare a statement of financial position at 31 March 20–8. [16]

	$
Motor vehicle	5 520
Trade receivables	11 600
Trade payables	6 320
Capital	18 280
Equipment	5 500
Inventory at 1 April 20–7	2 500
Wages and salaries	7 920
Purchases	26 320
Sales	42 680
Bank	220
Cash	160
Rent	1 320
Sales returns	1 640
Purchases returns	1 120
Fixtures and fittings	2 200
General expenses	800
Discounts allowed	2 080
Discounts received	1 480
Drawings	2 100

Inventory at 31 March 20–8 was valued at $3 200.

5 Coral runs a dance school which provides a range of different lessons to all ages. Her financial year ends on 31 October. She provided the following trial balance at 31 October 20–7:

	$	$
Income from lessons		98 500
Property	180 000	
Dance equipment	5 300	
Insurance	3 600	
Bank overdraft		475
Cash	125	
Loan interest	90	
Long term loan		10 000
Drawings	2 360	
Cleaning expenses	420	
Electricity	830	
Advertising	1 600	
Capital		

a Balance the trial balance and calculate the capital figure. [2]
b Prepare an income statement for the year ended 31 October 20–7. [7]
c Prepare a statement of financial position at 31 October 20–7. [8]

Revision checklist

In this chapter you have learnt:

- that statements of financial position are important to show what assets, liabilities and capital a business has on a specified date – the assets are items the business owns, liabilities are what is owed and the capital section is the amount invested by the owner

- the content of a statement of financial position: non-current assets, intangible assets, current assets, current liabilities, non-current liabilities and capital

- the inter-relationship of items in a statement of financial position, for example current assets are listed according to their closeness to cash

- that statements of financial position are the same for trading businesses and service businesses, but a service business will not have any inventory in the current assets section.

Chapter 10: Accounting rules

Learning summary

By the end of this chapter you should understand:

- the application of the following accounting principles: business entity, consistency, duality, going concern, historic cost, matching, materiality, money measurement, prudence and realisation
- the influence of international accounting standards and the following objectives in selecting accounting policies: comparability, relevance, reliability and understandability
- how to distinguish between and account for capital expenditure and revenue expenditure
- how to distinguish between and account for capital receipts and revenue receipts
- the effect on profit of incorrect treatment
- the effect on asset valuations of incorrect treatment
- the basis of the valuation of inventory at the lower of cost and net realisable value
- how to prepare simple inventory valuation statements
- the importance of valuation of inventory and the effect of an incorrect valuation of inventory on gross profit, profit for the year, equity and asset valuation.

TERMS

The **business entity principle** means that the business is treated as being completely separate from the owner of the business.

Capital expenditure is money spent on purchasing, improving or extending non-current assets.

A **capital receipt** is money received by a business from a source other than the normal trading activities.

The **consistency principle** means that accounting methods must be used consistently from one accounting period to the next.

The **going concern principle** means that the accounting records are maintained on the basis that the business will continue to operate for an indefinite period of time.

The **historic cost principle** means that all assets and expenses are initially recorded at their actual cost.

The **matching principle** means that the revenue of the accounting period is matched against the costs of the same period.

The **materiality principle** means that individual items which will not significantly affect either the profit or the assets of a business do not need to be recorded separately.

TERMS

The money measurement principle means that only information which can be expressed in terms of money can be recorded in the accounting records.

The principle of duality means that every transaction is recorded twice, once on the debit side and once on the credit side.

The prudence principle means that profits and assets should not be overstated, and losses and liabilities should not be understated.

The realisation principle means that revenue is only regarded as being earned when the legal title to goods passes from the seller to the buyer.

Revenue expenditure is money spent on running a business on a day-to-day basis.

A revenue receipt is money received by a business from normal trading activities.

TIPS

Ignore replacement cost in questions about inventory as this is not a valid method of valuing inventory.

Make sure you can define each of the principles and provide an example of each to illustrate your understanding.

If closing inventory is overstated then gross profit and profit for the year will both be overstated. Current assets on the statement of financial position will also be overstated.

Prudence is the overriding principle as it encourages accountants to take a cautious approach and not to overstate profits but to recognise losses as soon as possible.

Accounting rules and principles

The reasons for having rules and principles to follow in accounting is so that the financial statements produced are as accurate as possible and so that comparisons can then be made with other businesses and between years for the same business. Accountants will follow the same guidelines regardless of where in the world the financial statements are produced.

Going concern – unless we have knowledge to the contrary, we assume that the business will continue to trade in its present form for the foreseeable future. This means that we value all business assets at cost, not at what they would fetch if sold. If the business is going to continue, the assets will not be sold, so sale value is irrelevant.

Matching – expenses should be matched against the revenues that are earned as a result of those costs. So, even if we haven't yet paid for an expense, if it is to do with the current financial year, it needs to be included as an accrued expense. Similarly, if we have paid for rent/insurance which is for the next financial year, that needs to be subtracted as a prepaid expense.

Prudence – accountants provide for losses as soon as they are anticipated. In addition, they do not acknowledge profits until they are realised and all costs of earning revenue brought to account in the period are charged against that revenue.

Realisation – profits are normally recognised when, in legal terms, the title to the goods passes to the customer. Revenue should not be overstated by sales that have not been realised. The buyer has to be willing and able to pay in order for the sale to be recorded.

Consistency – once a firm has a fixed method for the accounting treatment of an item, similar items should be treated using the same method. For example, do not swap between straight line and reducing balance methods of depreciation. This allows comparisons to be made between different accounting years.

Business entity – this states that only the expenses and revenues relating to the business are recorded in the business books of account. Transactions involving the private affairs of the owner are not part of the business and should not be included in the business books. For example, the owner's private electricity or grocery bills should not be included as business expenditure. If the business cheque book is used to pay the owner's private mortgage, the amount should be included in the drawings account.

Materiality – this concept recognises that if we tried to be absolutely precise about everything it would cost the business considerable time and expense. As a rule, if a user of a financial statement would be misled by the exclusion or inclusion of an item of capital expenditure in the appropriate accounts, then that item is 'material'.

Historic cost – assets and liabilities are recorded in the financial statements at historic cost, i.e. the actual amount of the transaction involved.

Duality – for every debit entry there is a corresponding credit entry; every transaction has two aspects, a giving and a receiving.

Money measurement – information needs to be expressed in terms of money. You may have an experienced and loyal staff but this cannot be included as an asset on the statement of financial position.

If closing inventory is overstated then gross profit and profit for the year will both be overstated. Current assets on the statement of financial position will also be overstated.

Prudence is the overriding principle as it encourages accountants to take a cautious approach and not to overstate profits but to recognise losses as soon as possible.

Sample question

1. Roberto owns a building merchants on an industrial estate. The same sized property has recently sold for $180000 and yet Roberto continues to value his own property for the amount he originally paid for it five years ago, $50000.

    a State which principle this is an example of.

    Roberto has bought a new mirror to replace a broken one in his office. It cost $10.

    b Explain how this purchase should be dealt with in his financial statements and which principle helps him to make this decision.

> **Answer:**
> a   This is an example of the historic cost concept.
>
> b   The new mirror should be recorded in expenses on the income statement as it is an example of revenue expenditure. The principle is materiality as although the mirror is to be used in the business and is not for resale, it is replacing a broken mirror and its cost is small so it does not require placing on the statement of financial position and depreciating.

International accounting standards

International accounting standards are set by the International Accounting Standards Board and were introduced to bring comparability of success between companies and to produce financial statements that minimise creative accounting and promote consistency. The purpose of accounting standards is to address:

Comparability – information provided for one period must be comparable with that provided for the previous period and between companies. In order to achieve comparability, information must be given consistently from one period to another, and accounting policies such as depreciation used must be fully disclosed.

Relevance – financial statements need to be produced within a certain time frame so that they can be used to make decisions. The past events can help the users of the financial statements to adapt future plans or revisit decisions made in the light of the information provided.

Reliability – the information provided needs to be free from bias and from significant errors. The users should feel confident that objectivity has been used throughout, alongside all the other accounting principles, in order to produce the most accurate financial statements possible.

Understandability – users of financial statements are expected to have a reasonable knowledge of business and economic activities and accounting. This does not mean that a vital piece of information should be omitted just because it is complex.

Capital and revenue expenditure and receipts

It is important to differentiate between these transactions as they belong in different parts of the financial statements. Capital expenditure is recorded on the statement of financial position as it involves the purchasing or improving of non-current assets. Revenue expenditure is all other expenditure and is recorded on the income statement.

Revenue receipts arise from normal trading activities, such as selling goods and discounts received. Capital receipts are not recorded on the income statement except in the case of a sale of a non-current asset where a profit or loss may occur. If there is a profit, it is added after gross profit and if a loss, it is listed with expenses.

	Capital expenditure	Revenue expenditure	Capital receipt	Revenue receipt
Examples	Buying a motor vehicle	Purchasing goods for resale	Proceeds from the sale of a non-current asset	Revenue from sale of goods
	Building an extension on a property	Electricity	Receipt of loans	Rent received

Inventory valuation

The principle of prudence is applied when valuing inventory. If inventory is overvalued at the year end, gross profit and profit for the year will be overstated. This is why we value inventory at the lower of cost or net realisable value. Cost is the amount paid to obtain the inventory including any carriage inwards. Net realisable value is the estimated selling price less any costs to get the goods ready for resale, for example repairs or advertising.

It follows on that if profit for the year is overstated due to the closing inventory being overstated, then so too will the owner's equity be overstated. On the statement of financial position the current assets will be overstated due to the closing inventory, and this will be matched by the owner's equity being overstated due to the profit for the year being overstated. This will mean that the value of the business is higher than it should be which goes against the principle of prudence.

Progress check

1. What is the difference between capital and revenue expenditure?
2. State two examples of revenue receipts and two examples of capital receipts.
3. Why would a business wish to compare its financial statements with previous years and other similar businesses?
4. Explain how a business should value its assets.

Sample question

2. An item of inventory has an original cost of $28 and a replacement cost of $14. The costs of packing and delivery when the item is sold will amount to $5. It is expected to be sold for $32.

   State at which value it should be included in the financial statements.

   A $14

   B $19

   C $27

   D $28

   Answer: Inventory should be valued at the lower of cost or net realisable value. The answer is C as cost is $28 and net realisable value = selling price of $32 − packing and delivery cost of $5 = $27.

Examination-style questions

1. Give one example of capital expenditure. [1]

2. The purchase of inventory for resale has been treated as capital expenditure.

   Which item in the statement of financial position was understated? [1]

   A current assets
   B current liabilities
   C non-current assets
   D non-current liabilities

3. Prepare the following table by inserting a tick showing whether **each** transaction is revenue expenditure, a revenue receipt, capital expenditure or a capital receipt. The first one has been completed as an example. [5]

Transaction	Revenue Expenditure	Revenue Receipt	Capital Expenditure	Capital Receipt
Sold motor vehicle				✓
Paid rent				
Took out a ten-year bank loan				
Bought machinery to use in the business				
Sold inventory				
Repainted factory gates				

4. Prepare the table giving **one** principle which **has** been complied with if each proposed action is implemented. The first item has been completed as an example. [4]

Proposed action	Principle
Provide for trade debts which are probably irrecoverable	*Prudence*
Value inventory at lower of cost or net realisable value	
Continue to use straight line depreciation method	
The owner records money they take out of the business as drawings	
A new air conditioning unit is being recorded as a non-current asset	

5   A trader has calculated his draft gross profit for the year and then discovered the following:

- The closing inventory included a damaged item, A, which now has a selling price of $250 and needs repairs of $25 in order to be in saleable condition. The cost of item A was $300.

- Another item, B, which cost $80, can no longer be sold and must be disposed of.

Complete the following table by writing the amount which the gross profit, profit for the year and current assets currently are over or understated by. [3]

	Overstated	Understated
Gross profit for the year		
Profit for the year		
Current assets		

Revision checklist

In this chapter you have learnt:

- ☐ the main accounting principles are business entity, consistency, duality, going concern, historic cost, matching, materiality, money measurement, prudence and realisation

- ☐ the influence of international accounting standards on financial statements and the importance of comparability, relevance, reliability and understandability

- ☐ capital expenditure is recorded on the statement of financial position and revenue expenditure is recorded on the income statement; incorrect recording will result in incorrect profit and incorrect asset valuations

- ☐ capital receipts arise from non-trading activities and revenue receipts from normal trading activities

- ☐ inventory must be valued at the lower of cost or net realisable value and if this is incorrect it will have an effect on gross profit, profit for the year, equity and asset valuation.

Other payables and other receivables

Learning summary

By the end of this chapter you should understand:

- ☐ the importance of matching costs and revenues
- ☐ how to prepare ledger accounts to record accrued and prepaid expenses
- ☐ how to prepare ledger accounts to record accrued and prepaid incomes
- ☐ how to make adjustments for accrued and prepaid expenses and accrued and prepaid incomes.

TERMS

An **accrued expense** is an expense relating to a particular accounting period which is unpaid at the end of that period.

Accrued income is income relating to a particular accounting period which has not been received at the end of that period.

A **prepaid expense** is an expense paid during the financial year which relates to a future accounting period.

Prepaid income is income received during the financial year which relates to a future accounting period.

Accrued and prepaid expenses

The income and expenses which appear on an income statement are not the actual amounts which have been paid or received during the year. Instead, they are the amounts which should have been paid or received and this demonstrates the matching principle. Where an expense has been accrued, it means that some benefit or service has been received during the accounting period but has not yet been paid for. For example, wages which are usually paid after the worker has completed their necessary hours. These wages need to be included in this accounting period so will need adding to the wages on the income statement. The amount which is owed to the workers is entered on the statement of financial position as a current liability.

Item	Action to be taken
Accrued expenses (expenses incurred but not yet paid for)	1 Add amount of underpayment to the expenses in the trial balance, debit and amount is entered on the income statement
	2 Enter the amount of the underpayment in current liabilities, credit on the statement of financial position
Prepaid expenses (expenses paid for but not yet incurred)	1 Deduct amount of prepayment from the expenses figure in the trial balance, credit and amount is entered on the income statement
	2 Enter amount of prepayment in current assets, debit on the statement of financial position

Steps for completing ledger accounts with accrued expense or prepaid expense

1 Bring forward any accrued expense (credit side) or prepaid expense (debit side) from last year. Both are labelled as balance brought down.

2 Debit the account with cash and payments made via the bank account.

3 Credit the account with the amount incurred, i.e. what **should** have been paid. This is the transfer to the income statement.

4 Balance the account. The balancing figure is the accrued expense or prepaid expense. This is the balance carried down which then becomes the next accounting period's balance brought down.

Sample question

1 Liang pays for his electricity bill quarterly in arrears. At the start of the accounting year he owed $200. During the year ended 31 December 20–9 his payments for electricity were:

30 March	Paid in cash $220
2 July	Paid by cheque $190
4 October	Paid by credit transfer $340

An invoice for electricity for $150 was received on 4 January 20–0. This was for electricity expenses up to the end of December 20–9, but was not paid until 10 January 20–0.

a Prepare the electricity expenses account in Liang's nominal ledger for the year ended 31 December 20–9.

b Prepare a relevant extract from Liang's income statement for the year ended 31 December 20–9.

c Prepare a relevant extract from Liang's statement of financial position for the year ended 31 December 20–9.

Answer:

a

Liang
Nominal ledger
Electricity account

Date	Details	$	Date	Details	$
20–9			20–9		
Mar 30	Cash	220	Jan 1	Balance b/d	200
July 2	Bank	190	Dec 31	Income statement	700
Oct 4	Bank	340			
Dec 31	Balance c/d	150			
		900			900
			20–0		
			Jan 1	Balance b/d	150

b

Liang
Extract from income statement for the year ended 31 December 20–0

	$
Expenses – electricity	700

c

Liang
Extract from statement of financial position at 31 December 20–0

Current liabilities	$
Other payables	150

If there is more than one accrued expense then they can be added together and the total listed as other payables.

TIPS

If you have altered an expense then show the workings in brackets alongside the expense on the income statement and always show the new total and not just the workings.

The income statement shows the amount that should have been paid, not what was actually paid.

The amount recorded on the statement of financial position is just the amount owing at the year end (current liability) or the amount paid ahead (current asset).

Prepaid income is actually a current liability; if you receive an early birthday present it is not yours until your actual birthday and still belongs to the person who gave you the present.

Sample question

2. Thabo's financial year ended on 30 November 20–9.

   He had paid $3 000 on 31 May 20–9 for ten cleaning maintenance visits to run monthly from June 20–9 to March 20–0.

   How did this appear in his financial statements?

	Income statement	Statement of financial position
A	$1 200 expense	$1 800 current asset
B	$1 200 expense	$1 800 current liability
C	$1 800 expense	$1 200 current asset
D	$1 800 expense	$1 200 current liability

   Answer: The first stage is to find the monthly amount for cleaning which is $3 000/10 = $300. Then we need to multiply this by the number of months which concern the year ending 30 November 20–9. June to November is 6 months so $300 × 6 = $1 800. Subtract this $1 800 from $3 000 and this is $1 200 which is the amount of the prepaid expense, which is a current asset, so the correct answer is C.

Combined expense accounts

Some businesses may combine similar expenses into one account. The entries are identical but there may well be opening balances on both sides of the account as one expense may be prepaid and the other accrued. Or both accounts may have opening balances on the same side.

Sample question

3. Tariq is a trader. His financial year ends on 31 December. He maintains one combined account for rent and rates.

   On 1 January 20–8 two months' rent, $2 300, was prepaid and three months' rates, $1 200, was outstanding.

   During the year ended 31 December 20–8 the following payments were made by cheque:

	$
Rent 13 months to 31 March 20–9	14 950
Rates 16 months to 31 January 20–9	6 400

   Prepare the rent and rates account in the ledger of Tariq for the year ended 31 December 20–8. Balance the account and bring down the balances on 1 January 20–9.

Answer:

Tariq
Rent and rates account

Date	Details	$	Date	Details	$
20–8			20–8		
Jan 1	Balance b/d rent	2 300	Jan 1	Balance b/d rates	1 200
Dec 31	Bank rent	14 950	Dec 31	Income statement rent	13 800
	Bank rates	6 400		Income statement rates	4 800
				Balance c/d rent	3 450
				Balance c/d rates	400
20–9		23 650			23 650
Jan 1	Balance b/d rent	3 450			
	Balance b/d rates	400			

Starting with the rent, the opening balance is prepaid, so it is an asset and on the debit side of the account. The actual payment via the bank account was $14 950 so this would be credited in the bank account and then debited to the expense account. This payment covers 13 months so $\frac{14950}{13}$ = 1 150, so then multiply this by 12 to find the income statement amount, which is what should have been paid, $13 800. The payment covers up to 31 March, 3 months, so the prepaid expense is 1 150 × 3 = $ 3 450. This will appear on the statement of financial position as a current asset.

The rates starts off an accrued expense on the credit side because it is a liability and is owed. Tariq then pays $6 400 which covers 16 months. $\frac{6400}{16}$ = 400. The income statement amount needs to cover 12 months, so 400 × 12 = $4 800. One month has been prepaid which is $400. Both accounts end up with a debit balance as both expenses have now been prepaid.

Accrued and prepaid income

In the same way that a business may pay ahead for some expenses or later for others, then the same can happen in terms of its income from sources other than trading. For example, if the business rents out part of its property, it may ask the tenant to pay ahead. This prepaid income does not belong to the business until the date it concerns so it is still essentially the tenant's money. Accrued income operates in the same way as a sale on credit. The income is included even though the money hasn't been received and the amount owed is a current asset.

Item	Action to be taken
Accrued income (income that has been earned but not yet paid for)	1 Add amount of underpayment to the income in the trial balance, credit and amount is entered on the income statement
	2 Enter the amount of the underpayment in current assets, debit on the statement of financial position
Prepaid income (income received but not yet due)	1 Deduct amount of prepayment from the income figure in the trial balance, debit and amount is entered on the income statement
	2 Enter amount of prepayment in current liabilities, credit on the statement of financial position

Progress check

1. What is the difference between accrued expense and accrued income?
2. How does the matching principle impact on the income statement and statement of financial position?
3. Why is prepaid income classified as a current liability on the statement of financial position?

Examination-style questions

1. Saffy is a hairdresser who rents her property.

    Until 31 December 20–8 the rent was $2 000 a month. From 1 January 20–9 the rent was $2 300 a month.

    a Calculate the rent for the year ended 30 September 20–9. [1]

    The balance on Saffy's rent account on 1 October 20–8 was $2 000 credit. During the year she made three payments of rent by credit transfer, as follows:

	$
3 October 20–8	12 000
2 January 20–9	8 500
4 May 20–9	10 500

    b State what the balance on 1 October 20–8 represented. [1]

    c Prepare Saffy's rent account for the year ended 30 September 20–9. Balance the account and bring down the balance on 1 October 20–9. [5]

2 Sheniya is preparing her financial statements. She provides the following information:

| 1 November 20–8 | Rent receivable account | $4 200 debit |

The bank account contained the following entries:

Receipts		
31 December 20–8	Rent received by cheque $12 200	
31 March 20–9	Rent received by credit transfer $9 150	
Payments		
12 February 20–9	Refund for overpayment of rent receivable $500	

The rent receivable amounts to $20 000 a year.

Prepare the rent receivable account for the year ended 31 October 20–9. Make the transfer to the income statement and bring down the balance on 1 November 20–9. [5]

3 The following is a summary of information to be entered into the rent and rates expense account for Nigel for the year ended 30 November 20–8:

		$
1 December 20–7	Rent accrued brought forward	3 800
1 December 20–7	Rates prepaid brought forward	1 050
30 November 20–8	Total cheques paid for rent	18 500
30 November 20–8	Standing orders paid for rates	9 200
30 November 20–8	Rent prepaid carried forward	1 200
30 November 20–8	Rates prepaid carried forward	850

a Prepare the rent and rates expenses account for the year ended 30 November 20–8. Make the transfers to the income statement and bring down the balances on 1 December 20–8. [8]

b Prepare a relevant extract from Nigel's statement of financial position for the year ended 30 November 20–8. [2]

4 Kieran's statement of financial position includes the following:

i   an amount owed to Kieran for a service he has provided but not yet been paid for

ii an amount paid by Kieran for a service which Kieran has not yet received

iii the value of a service received by Kieran for which payment has not yet been made.

Which item(s) are included in 'other receivables'?

A i and ii

B i only

C ii and iii

D iii only

5 Nabeegh is a retailer and owns a computer store. His financial year ends on 31 December. He provided the following trial balance on 31 December 20–7:

	$	$
Purchases and revenue	92 500	128 450
Discounts	2 200	1 800
Returns	680	946
Insurance	820	
Rent received		5 200
Wages	32 000	
Trade payables and trade receivables	7 200	6 690
Property	195 000	
Bank overdraft		2 500
Fixtures and fittings	3 690	
Office expenses	746	
Capital		196 500
4% 6 year loan from PG Finance		8 000
Drawings	4 500	
Inventory 1 January 20–7	10 750	
	350 086	350 086

Additional information:

At 31 December 20–7:
- Inventory was valued at $11 300.
- Rent receivable owed amounted to $1 350.
- Insurance prepaid amounted to $355.
- Wages accrued amounted to $2 380.
- A whole year's interest on the loan is outstanding.

a Prepare an income statement for the year ended 31 December 20–7. [16]
b Prepare a statement of financial position at 31 December 20–7. [12]

Revision checklist

In this chapter you have learnt:

- ☐ the importance of matching costs and revenues to their relevant accounting period
- ☐ how to prepare ledger accounts to record accrued (current liability) and prepaid expenses (current assets)
- ☐ how to prepare ledger accounts to record accrued (current asset) and prepaid income (current liability)
- ☐ how to make adjustments for accrued and prepaid expenses and accrued and prepaid income, so that what should have been paid or received is recorded on the income statement and the amount accrued or prepaid is recorded on the statement of financial position.

Accounting for depreciation and disposal of non-current assets

Chapter 12

Learning summary

By the end of this chapter you should understand:

- how to define depreciation
- the reasons for accounting for depreciation
- the straight line, reducing balance and revaluation methods of depreciation
- how to prepare ledger accounts for the provision of depreciation
- how to prepare ledger accounts to record the sale of non-current assets, including the use of disposal accounts
- how to make adjustments for provision for depreciation using the straight line, reducing balance and revaluation methods.

TERMS

Depreciation is an estimate of the loss in value of a non-current asset over its expected working life.

The **net book value** of a non-current asset is the cost price minus the total depreciation to date.

The **residual value** is the value of a non-current asset at the end of its useful life.

The **reducing balance method of depreciation** is where the depreciation charged each year decreases as it is calculated on the net book value rather than the cost.

The **revaluation method of depreciation** is where the opening and closing value of a non-current asset are compared (after adjusting for any additions during the year) to determine the depreciation for the year.

The **straight line method** of depreciation is where the same amount of depreciation is charged each year.

Depreciation and its causes

Depreciation is an estimated amount representing the value lost whilst using a non-current asset. Although it appears on the income statement in the expenses section it is not an actual cost which is paid. It is linked to the matching principle as it is an attempt to fairly reflect how much of the non-current asset was consumed in the accounting year. It is just the depreciation for the year which appears on the income statement and then on the statement of financial position, all of the depreciation so far is subtracted from the original cost of the asset to show a more realistic value of the asset following the principle of prudence. The four main causes of depreciation are:

- physical deterioration – due to wear and tear, or rust, rot, etc.
- economic reasons – original asset can no longer perform its function or a newer version is available.
- time – a lease, for example, on property may have a certain amount of years attached.
- depletion – the asset will run out, e.g. oil well.

Methods of depreciation

There are three methods which you need to learn:

- straight line method
- reducing balance method
- revaluation method.

An exact figure for depreciation can only be determined when a non-current asset is sold.

For example, if a business buys a machine for $13 000 and disposes of it five years later for $3 000, the total depreciation charge would be $10 000.

Accountants have to make an estimate and to do this they need to know:

- the purchase price of the asset (historic cost)
- its expected useful life (how long the business will own it for)
- its estimated disposal value (how much it is worth at the end of its useful life – residual/scrap value).

Straight line method of depreciation

1. For this method, the number of years of use is estimated. The cost is then divided by the number of years to give the depreciation charge each year.

    For example, if equipment was bought for $22 000 and it was expected to be kept for four years and be sold for $2 000, the depreciation charge would be:

    $$\frac{\text{Cost} - \text{Residual value}}{\text{Number of expected years of use}} = \frac{22\,000 - 2\,000}{4} = \$5\,000 \text{ each year}$$

    If there is no residual value then the calculation is simply cost divided by the number of expected years.

2. The other method simply uses a percentage of the cost. So, using the above example, the depreciation at 10% would be $2 200. The residual value is ignored for this approach.

    This method is useful for assets which provide equal benefits for each year of their useful lives, such as fixtures and fittings, property and equipment.

Reducing balance method of depreciation

Instead of using the same amount of depreciation each year, this method recognises that with some assets, such as motor vehicles and machinery, the greater benefits are in the first few years and then repairs and replacements are needed. The net book value (cost – all depreciation to date) is used instead of the cost. This means the amount of depreciation reduces each year.

Sample question

1. A vehicle is purchased for $30 000. Depreciation is to be provided at 20% per annum, using the reducing balance method. Calculate the annual depreciation charge for the first three years of ownership and the net book value at the end of each year.

Answer:

Year	Cost $	Depreciation $	Net book value $
1	30 000	6 000	24 000
2	30 000	4 800	19 200
3	30 000	3 840	15 360

The depreciation for year 1 is 20% of the cost. After the first year it is the net book value figure which is used each time to calculate the depreciation charge for the year. The depreciation for the year will appear in the expenses section of the income statement and the cost minus all depreciation so far will appear in the non-current assets section of the statement of financial position.

Revaluation method of depreciation

This method is used when it would be too time consuming to depreciate the items such as cooking pots in a hotel, loose tools in a factory or small items of equipment in an office. The assets are valued at the end of the year and compared with the previous valuation and the difference is the depreciation.

	Advantage	Disadvantage
Straight line method	Easy to calculate	Have to estimate useful life and residual value
Reducing balance method	Useful where greater benefits in earlier years	Depreciation has to be recalculated each year
Revaluation method	No complex calculation	Based on personal opinion so may not be accurate

Recording depreciation in the ledger

There are two ledger accounts involved, the non-current asset account which is a debit and records the actual cost paid for the asset, and the provision for depreciation account which is always a credit as it is the opposite to an asset as it is reducing the value of the asset. The difference between these two accounts is the net book value of the asset.

Sample question

2 Using the information from Sample question 1, Keeya wishes to record the following in her nominal ledger. Her financial year ends on 31 May. On 1 June 20–5 she purchased a motor vehicle for $30 000 and paid by cheque. Depreciation is to be provided at 20% per annum, using the reducing balance method. Prepare Keeya's nominal ledger accounts for each of the years ended 31 May 20–6, 20–7 and 20–8.

Answer:

Keeya
Nominal ledger
Motor vehicle account

Date	Details	$	Date	Details	$
20–5					
June 1	Bank	30 000			

This does not need balancing at the end of each year as there is only one entry.

Provision for depreciation of motor vehicle account

Date	Details	$	Date	Details	$
20–6			20–6		
May 31	Balance c/d	6 000	May 31	Income statement	6 000
		6 000			6 000
			June 1	Balance b/d	6 000
20–7			20–7		
May 31	Balance c/d	10 800	May 31	Income statement	4 800
		10 800			10 800
			June 1	Balance b/d	10 800
20–8			20–8		
May 31	Balance c/d	14 640	May 31	Income statement	3 840
		14 640			14 640
			June 1	Balance b/d	14 640

If the straight line method had been used then each year the income statement amount would be the same. The layout is identical for both methods.

3 Keeya's financial year ends on 31 May.

On 1 June 20–8 she purchased loose tools costing $3 300 and paid by cheque. She decided to revalue the loose tools at the end of each year. On 31 May 20–9 the loose tools were valued at $3 000.

Prepare the loose tools account in the nominal ledger for the year ended 31 May 20–9.

Answer:

Keeya
Nominal ledger
Loose tools account

Date	Details	$	Date	Details	$
20–8			20–9		
June 1	Bank	3 300	May 31	Income statement	300
				Balance c/d	3 000
		3 300			3 300
20–9					
June 1	Balance b/d	3 000			

The depreciation charge is the difference between the amount the loose tools were purchased for and the amount they were valued at the end of the financial year, so $300.

Recording depreciation in the financial statements

This year's depreciation is an expense on the income statement and the total depreciation to date is subtracted from the cost of the non-current asset on the statement of financial position to provide the net book value.

Sample question

4 Below is an extract from the trial balance for Guang at 30 September 20–8. Guang uses the straight line method of depreciation at 20% per annum.

	Debit $	Credit $
Fixtures and fittings	150 000	
Provision for depreciation		90 000

Prepare a relevant extract from Guang's income statement for the year ended 30 September 20–8 and from his statement of financial position at 30 September 20–8.

Answer:

Guang
Extract from income statement for the year ended 30 September 20–8

	$
Expenses – depreciation of fixtures and fittings	30 000

Multiply the cost of $150 000 by 20% to find the year's depreciation of $30 000.

Guang
Extract from statement of financial position at 30 September 20–8

Non-current assets	$ Cost	$ Accumulated depreciation	$ Net book value
Fixtures and fittings	150 000	120 000	30 000

The accumulated depreciation is the provision for depreciation from the trial balance added to this year's depreciation charge. Always show the netted off figure for the net book value.

Disposal of non-current assets

The sale of a non-current asset is not recorded in the sales account as it is a capital receipt in the same way that a purchase of a non-current asset is capital expenditure instead of revenue expenditure. A separate account, known as a disposal of non-current assets, is set up. It records the initial cost of the non-current asset, the accumulated depreciation for the non-current asset and then the amount received by cash or bank. The account essentially compares the net book value of time of sale with the proceeds from the sale to calculate profit or loss. Both a profit or loss are recorded on the income statement; the profit (means we overestimated the amount of depreciation) is added to the gross profit and the loss (means we underestimated the amount of depreciation) is included in the expenses section. The actual money received is debited to the cash or cash equivalents account.

Sample question

5   Keeya's financial year ends on 31 May. On 1 June 20–5 she purchased a motor vehicle for $30 000 by cheque. She decided to depreciate the motor vehicle using the reducing balance method. On 1 June 20–8 the provision for depreciation of motor vehicles account showed a credit balance of $14 640. Keeya sold the motor vehicle for $14 500 to be paid by credit transfer by Car Trader Ltd.

Prepare Keeya's nominal ledger accounts for the year ended 31 May 20–9.

Answer:

Keeya
Nominal ledger
Motor vehicle account

Date	Details	$	Date	Details	$
20–5			20–8		
June 1	Bank	30 000	June 1	Disposal	30 000
		30 000			30 000

Provision for depreciation of motor vehicle account

Date	Details	$	Date	Details	$
20–8			20–8		
June 1	Disposal	14 640	June 1	Balance b/d	14 640
		14 640			14 640

Disposal of motor vehicle account

Date	Details	$	Date	Details	$
20–8			20–8		
June 1	Vehicle	30 000	June 1	Provision for depreciation	14 640
				Bank	14 500
			20–9		
			May 31	Income statement	860
		30 000			30 000

The loss of $860 will appear in the expenses section of the income statement.

TIPS

Ensure you label which non-current asset the depreciation belongs to on the income statement.

It is depreciation for the year which belongs on the income statement, and all depreciation which has occurred so far which is recorded on the statement of financial position which comes from the provision for depreciation account.

Progress check

1. Name the account which is opened when a non-current asset is sold.
2. What type of assets are depreciated using the revaluation method?
3. What is the double entry for a book-keeper to record a depreciation charge for the year?

Examination-style questions

1. Marcus is setting up his own business and is confused about which method of depreciation he should use for his machinery. Explain the three methods of depreciation and advise Marcus as to which method he should choose. [8]

2. On 1 January 20–7 Now Ltd had fixtures and fittings which had cost $42 000.

   On 1 April 20–7 it paid by cheque for new fixtures and fittings, $15 200, and sold old fixtures and fittings with an original cost of $3 100. There was no profit or loss on this disposal.

   Now Ltd provides for depreciation on fixtures and fittings at a rate of 20% per annum on the straight line basis.

   It provides a full year's depreciation in the year of purchase and none in the year of disposal.

   a Prepare the fixtures and fittings for the year ended 31 December 20–7. Balance the account and bring down the balance on 1 January 20–8. [5]

   b Calculate the depreciation charge for the year ended 31 December 20–8. [2]

3. Shavaiz depreciates motor vehicles at the rate of 30% per annum using the reducing balance method. He provides a full year's depreciation in the year of purchase and none in the year of disposal. His accounting year end is 31 December.

   He purchased a motor vehicle for $15 000 on 1 March 20–7 and sold it on 27 June 20–9 for $8 250 cash. On the same date he bought a new motor vehicle for $19 500, paying by cheque.

   a Calculate the depreciation which had been provided on the old motor vehicle at the date of disposal. [3]

   b Prepare the following ledger accounts for the year ended 31 December 20–9: motor vehicles account, provision for depreciation of motor vehicles account and motor vehicle disposal account. [14]

4. Amina's financial year end is December 31. She bought a delivery van in March 20–1 for $8 000. She provided for depreciation using the reducing balance method at 20% per annum and then sold the delivery van during 20–4 for $3 500. A full year's depreciation is charged in the year of purchase and none in the year of disposal.

   Calculate the profit or loss on disposal. [1]

   A $596   C $3 904

   B $3 500   D $4 096

5. Uday owns a sportswear shop. His financial year ends on 31 May. He provided the following trial balance at 31 May 20–7:

	$	$
Property	180 000	
Fixtures and fittings	4 500	
Provision for depreciation for fixtures and fittings		1 800
Delivery van	15 000	
Provision for depreciation for delivery van		7 320
Purchases	76 500	
Revenue		185 000
Inventory at 1 June 20–6	10 350	
Trade receivables	3 480	
Trade payables		1 860
Carriage inwards	1 040	
Commission receivable		3 875
General expenses	2 600	
Motor expenses	1 920	
Wages	42 790	
Cash and cash equivalents	4 260	
Discounts allowed	635	
Discounts received		1 800
Lighting and heating	1 080	
Capital		147 000
Drawings	4 500	
	348 655	348 655

Additional information:

- Inventory at 31 May 20–7 was valued at $9 700.
- General expenses of $280 had been prepaid.
- Wages accrued amounted to $450.
- Commission receivable prepaid, $600.
- Fixtures and fittings are being depreciated at 10% per annum using the straight line method.
- Motor vehicles are being depreciated at 20% per annum using the reducing balance method.
- No entries have been made for the sale of fixtures and fittings for cash on 30 March 20–7 for $200. They had originally been purchased during the year ended 31 May 20–4 for $450.
- A full year's depreciation is provided in the year of purchase of non-current assets and none in the year of disposal.

a Prepare an income statement for the year ended 31 May 20–7. [15]

b Prepare a statement of financial position at 31 May 20–7. [12]

Revision checklist

In this chapter you have learnt:

- ☐ depreciation represents the fall in value of non-current assets
- ☐ the reasons for accounting for depreciation are physical deterioration, economic reasons, passage of time and depletion
- ☐ the methods of depreciation – straight line uses the cost of the non-current asset, reducing balance uses the net book value of the non-current asset and revaluation compares the value at the start and end of the year of the non-current assets
- ☐ how to prepare ledger accounts for the provision of depreciation and that the opening balance is always a credit balance
- ☐ how to prepare ledger accounts to record the sale of non-current assets, including the use of disposal accounts in order to calculate profit or loss on disposal
- ☐ how to make adjustments for provision for depreciation using the straight line, reducing balance and revaluation methods.

Chapter 13

Irrecoverable debts and provisions for doubtful debts

Learning summary

By the end of this chapter you should understand:

- the meaning of irrecoverable debts and recovery of debts written off
- how to prepare ledger accounts to record irrecoverable debts
- how to prepare ledger accounts to record recovery of debts written off
- the reasons for maintaining a provision for doubtful debts
- how to prepare ledger accounts to record the creation of, and adjustments to, a provision for doubtful debts
- how to make adjustments for irrecoverable debts and provisions for doubtful debts.

TERMS

A **debt written off** may be recovered if a credit customer pays some, or all, of the amount owed, after the amount was written off.

An **irrecoverable debt** is an amount owing to a business which will not be paid by the credit customer.

A **provision for doubtful debts** is an estimate of the amount which a business will lose in a financial year because of irrecoverable debts.

Irrecoverable debts

If a business provides customers with credit then it runs the risk that some customers may never pay for goods that have been provided to them. You may think the simple solution is not to offer credit, however, if your competitors offer credit then there is little choice. The key is to minimise the amount of irrecoverable debts by having tight credit control. This means sending sales invoices promptly, sending statements of accounts monthly which summarise transactions and keeping an eye on how much credit the customers take.

When the debt is written off	Debit – irrecoverable debts account
	Credit – customer account
At the year-end	Debit – expenses on the income statement
	Credit – irrecoverable debts account

Irrecoverable debts are classified as an expense as although a business has not physically spent money, it has suffered as a consequence. Rather than subtract the amount from revenue, 'irrecoverable debts' has its own entry in the expenses section. This is an application of the principle of prudence as the business no longer has the asset of the trade receivable so the current assets are not overstated.

Recovery of debts written off

Sometimes a debt may be written off as irrecoverable and then the customer is in a position to repay what they owe. Perhaps the customer is in a position to restart trading and wants to buy goods once more.

When the amount is received	Debit – cash book
	Credit – debts recovered account
At the year-end	Debit – debts recovered account
	Credit – income statement, add to gross profit in other income section

Some businesses may offset recovered debts to the irrecoverable debts account. It is useful to keep the two accounts separate so a more accurate picture of the success of credit control can be achieved.

Provision for doubtful debts

This is different to irrecoverable debts as the provision is a 'just in case' action rather than recording a trade receivable unable to pay.

An initial creation of a provision for doubtful debts would be as follows:

1. A business, at the end of the financial year, estimates the percentage of its trade receivables which may not pay, e.g. 2%.
2. The provision is calculated. For example, if receivables are $9 800, at 2% the provision is $196.
3. Debit the income statement in expenses.
4. Credit the provision for doubtful debts account.
5. List the amount in the income statement like any other expense and subtract the amount from trade receivables in the current assets section on the statement of financial position.

Adjustments to provision for doubtful debts

Once a provision for doubtful debts has been created it can be adjusted upwards or downwards depending on the amount of trade receivables, state of the economy, etc.

Increase in provision for doubtful debts is recorded in the expenses section of the income statement.

Decrease in provision for doubtful debts is added to the gross profit in the other income section of the income statement.

The new full amount is subtracted from the trade receivables on the statement of financial position. It is the change which goes on the income statement.

Sample questions

1. On 31 December 20–8 Yaron created a provision for doubtful debts of $1 250. During the year ended 31 December 20–8 he wrote off debts totally, $720.

   On 31 December 20–9 his trade receivables amounted to $32 000. He decided to maintain the provision for doubtful debts at the rate of 5% of the trade receivables.

   a Prepare the irrecoverable debts account and the provision for doubtful debts account in Yaron's nominal ledger for the year ended 31 December 20–9.

   b Prepare a relevant extract from Yaron's income statement for the year ended 31 December 20–9.

   c Prepare a relevant extract from Yaron's statement of financial position at 31 December 20–9.

Answer:

a

Yaron
Nominal ledger
Irrecoverable debts account

Date	Details	$	Date	Details	$
20–9			20–9		
Dec 31	Trade receivables written off	720	Dec 31	Income statement	720
		720			720

Provision for doubtful debts account

Date	Details	$	Date	Details	$
20–9			20–9		
Dec 31	Balance c/d	1 600	Jan 1	Balance b/d	1 250
			Dec 31	Income statement	350
		1 600	20–0		1 600
			Jan 1	Balance b/d	1 600

b

Yaron
Extract from income statement for the year ended 31 December 20–9

	$
Expenses – irrecoverable debts	720
Increase in provision for doubtful debts	350

c

Extract from statement of financial position at 31 December 20–9

	$	$
Current assets		
Trade receivables	32 000	
Less Provision for doubtful debts	1 600	30 400

Note that it is the change in the provision which is entered on the income statement and the new provision is subtracted from trade receivables on the statement of financial position.

2 A trader provided the following information:

	At 31 August 20–7	At 31 August 20–8
Trade receivables	$62 000	$75 000
Rate of provision for doubtful debts	8%	6%

Which entry for provision of doubtful debts appeared in his income statement for the year ended 31 August 20–8?

A $460 as an expense

B $460 as an income

C $1 500 as an expense

D $1 500 as an income

Answer: The original provision is 62 000 × 0.08 = 4 960. The new provision is 75 000 × 0.06 = 4 500. The provision has fallen by $460 so the answer is B as this would appear as income on the income statement.

3 To help with credit control, many firms produce an aged schedule of receivables at the end of each month. This analyses individual receivable balances into the time that the amount has been owing.

Days outstanding	Trade receivables $
Current (up to 30 days)	5 000
31 to 60	7 500
61 to 90	12 300
91 and over	1 200

Calculate the provision for doubtful debts – 75% on debts outstanding for over 91 days, 40% on debts 61–90 days, 10% on debts 31–60 days. No provision on current debts.

Answer: 75% of $1 200 is $900, 40% of $12 300 is $4 920, 10% of $7 500 is $750.

Total provision for doubtful debts is $6 570.

> **TIPS**
>
> It is the change in provision for doubtful debts which appears on the income statement and the new full closing balance on the account is subtracted from trade receivables on the statement of financial position.
>
> If irrecoverable debts appear in the trial balance then they have already been subtracted from trade receivables. If they appear as additional information then they need debiting to the irrecoverable debts account and the relevant trade receivable accounts needs crediting.

Progress check

1 Name one accounting principle that supports the use of a provision for doubtful debts.
2 Where do recoverable debts appear on the income statement?
3 What is an aged schedule of trade receivables used for?
4 Why can a provision for doubtful debts appear as an income item or an expense item on the statement of financial position?

Examination-style questions

1 Usmaan maintains a provision for doubtful debts at 6% of his trade receivables. The following account appeared in his ledger:

Usmaan
Provision for doubtful debts account

Date	Details	$	Date	Details	$
20–8			20–7		
July 31	Balance c/d	1 050	Aug 1	Balance b/d	850
			20–8		
			July 31	Income statement	200
		1 050			1 050
			Aug 1	Balance b/d	1 050

Which statement is correct? [1]

A Irrecoverable debts recovered during the year amounted to $200.

B Irrecoverable debts during the year amounted to $200.

C Total trade receivables decreased during the year.

D Total trade receivables increased during the year.

2 On 1 June 20–8 the balance on the provision for doubtful debts account was $2 300.

Rose maintains a provision for doubtful debts at 5% and her total trade receivables for the year ended 31 May 20–9 are $55 000.

Prepare the provision for doubtful debts account for the year ended 31 May 20–9. Balance the account and bring down the balance on 1 June 20–9. [4]

3 At the year ended 31 December 20–7, Kian Ltd had a trade receivable balance of $230 000 and a provision for doubtful debts of $11 500. At the year ended December 20–8, trade receivables had increased to $350 000.

After reviewing its position at the year end, the company's finance director made the following discoveries (none of which have yet been dealt with):

i   One of Kian's credit customers, Fox Ltd, has gone into liquidation owing $4 800.

ii Kian Ltd received $2 500 from HLP Ltd (a trade receivable that had previously been written off as irrecoverable).

The finance director has decided to make a provision for doubtful debts at the same rate as the year ended 31 December 20–7.

Prepare the accounts for Kian: irrecoverable debts, debts recovered and provision for doubtful debts for the year ended 31 December 20–8. Balance or total the accounts or make an appropriate year-end transfer as necessary.

Prepare a statement of financial position extract and an income statement extract for Kian Ltd for the year ended 31 December 20–8. [16]

4 Destiny Diva is a make-up artist.

The following trial balance is provided at 31 August 20–8:

	$	$
Capital		25 000
Drawings	13 000	
Motor vehicle at cost	12 000	
Provision for depreciation of motor vehicle		2 400
Office equipment at cost	5 000	
Provision for depreciation of office equipment		1 000
Trade receivables	4 500	
Loan (repayable 20–0)		5 000
Irrecoverable debts	120	
Provision for doubtful debts		180
Fees from clients		14 500
Insurance	1 300	
Make-up expenses	4 650	
Motor vehicle expenses	1 580	
Cash	120	
Bank	5 810	
	48 080	48 080

The following information is supplied:

i At 31 August 20–8:

- insurance prepaid amounted to $250
- make-up expenses owing amounted to £320
- loan interest owing amounted to $200.

ii The motor vehicle is being depreciated at the rate of 20% per annum using the reducing balance method.

iii The office equipment is being depreciated at the rate of 10% per annum using the straight line method.

iv The provision for doubtful debts is maintained at 3% of the trade receivables.

a Prepare the income statement of Destiny Diva for the year ended 31 August 20–8. [10]

b Prepare the statement of financial position of Destiny Diva at 31 August 20–8. [11]

5 Riley is a trader selling goods on credit. Her financial year ends on 30 June.

The balances on her books on 1 May 20–8 included the following:

	$
Provision for doubtful debts	1 450
Arthur, a credit customer	1 200

Riley's transactions for the year ended 31 May 20–9 included the following:

July 6	Received a bank transfer from Arthur to settle his outstanding balance.
August 20	Sold goods on credit to Arthur, list price $500, less trade discount of 10%.
September 1	Received $200 from Denise whose account had been written off three years ago.
March 24	Arthur was declared bankrupt and his account was written off.
May 31	Decided to reduce her provision for doubtful debts to $1 200

Prepare the accounts for Arthur, irrecoverable debts, debts recovered and provision for doubtful debts for the year ended 31 May 20–9. Balance or total the accounts or make an appropriate year-end transfer as necessary. [12]

Revision checklist

In this chapter you have learnt:

- that irrecoverable debts occur when a trade receivable is no longer able to pay what they owe and recovery of debts written off occurs if a previous irrecoverable debt is later paid

- irrecoverable debts are a credit in the trade receivable account, debited to the irrecoverable debt account and then finally become an expense on the income statement

- recovery of debts written off are a debit to the bank or cash account, credited to the recovery of debts written off account and then are added to gross profit in the income statement

- a provision for doubtful debts recognises the possibility that some of the existing trade receivables may be unable to pay what they owe

- the opening balance for a provision for doubtful debts account is always on the credit side as it is the opposite to trade receivables since it reduces the amount trade receivables owe the business

- it is possible for a provision for doubtful debts to increase or decrease; the change is recorded on the income statement and the new balance is subtracted from trade receivables in the current assets section on the statement of financial position.

Section 4

Chapter 14

Bank reconciliation statements

Learning summary

By the end of this chapter you should understand:

- the use and purpose of a bank statement
- how to update the cash book for bank charges, bank interest paid and received, correction of errors, credit transfers, direct debits, dividends and standing orders
- the purpose of, and be able to prepare, a bank reconciliation statement to include bank errors, uncredited deposits and unpresented cheques.

TERMS

A **bank reconciliation statement** is a document prepared by a business to explain why the updated bank balance in the cash book does not agree with the balance on the bank statement.

A **bank statement** is a copy of a customer's account in the books of the bank which is sent to the customer at regular intervals.

Use and purpose of a bank reconciliation

A bank reconciliation involves looking at the same account, the bank account, from two different perspectives: the bank and the business. If transactions happened instantaneously and no one ever made errors then there would be no need to carry out a bank reconciliation, as the balance of the bank account would be the same from both viewpoints. The fact is that due to timing issues and amounts not yet accounted for, there is frequently a difference between the balance according to the cash book (the business) and the balance according to the bank statement (the bank). What we have to do is essentially merge the two together to produce the most accurate bank balance which can then be included on our statement of financial position at the year end.

Reasons for differences

Timing differences – cheques not yet presented, that have been entered on the credit side of the cash book but have not yet passed through the bank clearing system, do not yet appear on the bank statement. In a similar way, amounts not yet credited have been entered on the debit side of the cash book, cheques and cash that the business has received but due to the time delay in banking are not yet on the bank statement.

Items not recorded in the cash book – bank charges and interest; often a business will not know the amount of interest it has earned or the interest and charges it needs to pay until it receives the bank statement.

Dishonoured cheques – this will be returned to the business due to insufficient funds in the bank account of the person paying the cheque.

Amounts paid directly into and out of the bank – this is becoming the most common way for a business to both pay and receive money via the bank account as there is no time delay or a chance to forget to make the payment. Examples include credit transfers, standing orders and direct debits. These could be into or out of the business. A business may have shares in another company and receive dividends so these will need to be debited to the cash book.

How to complete a bank reconciliation

1 Start by matching items which appear both on the bank statement and cash book. Tick them off if they are the same. Remember to ignore dates in terms of matching as these will usually not be the same.

2 Update the cash book by entering items in the cash book which are not ticked on the bank statement. These will be items such as direct debits, credit transfers or bank charges and interest.

3 Correct any errors in the cash book where the amounts in the two places do not match. Unless otherwise instructed you should assume that it is the business which has made the error and not the bank.

4 Balance the cash book and carry down the balance. This amount will then appear in the statement of financial position.

5 You are then ready to complete the bank reconciliation statement.

The reconciliation can be started with either the cash book or bank statement balance.

Bank reconciliation statement at the date it is prepared

- Balance at bank shown in cash book
- Add unpresented cheques (look for unticked items on the credit side of the cash book)
- Less amounts not yet credited (this time it is the unticked items on the debit side of the cash book)
- Balance at bank shown on bank statement

Sample questions

1 The bank columns of Ebele's cash book for the month of March 20–7 are as follows:

Cash book (bank columns)

Date	Details	$	Date	Details	$
20–7			20–7		
Mar 1	Balance b/d	2 150	Mar 4	Sleaford Sleepers	412
6	Longdendale Ltd	560	14	Purchases 0326	945
17	Tamar Valley	395	23	Foo Foo 0327	1 113
28	Sales	3 264	31	Balance c/d	3 899
		6 369			6 369
Apr 1	Balance b/d	3 899			

Ebele received the following bank statement for the month of March 20–7:

Date	Details	Debit $	Credit $	Balance $	
20–7					
Mar 1	Balance			2 150	Cr
4	Bank charges	85		2 065	Cr
6	Sleaford Sleepers	412		1 653	Cr
8	Longdendale Ltd		560	2 213	Cr
10	Rent standing order	800		1 413	Cr
17	Cheque no 0326	954		459	Cr
23	Electricity direct debit	68		391	Cr
28	Bank interest		32	423	Cr

a Prepare an updated cash book, balance the bank account and bring down the balance on 1 April 20–7.

b Prepare a bank reconciliation statement at 31 March 20–7.

Answer:

a The first stage is to tick off the matching items as below:

Cash book (bank columns)

Date	Details	$	Date	Details	$
20–7			20–7		
Mar 1	Balance b/d	2 150	Mar 4	Sleaford Sleepers	412 ✓
6	Longdendale Ltd	560 ✓	14	Purchases 0326	945
17	Tamar Valley	395	23	Foo Foo 0327	1 113
28	Sales	3 264			
			31	Balance c/d	3 899
		6 369			6 369
Apr 1	Balance b/d	3 899			

Date	Details	Debit $	Credit $	Balance $	
20–7					
Mar 1	Balance			2150	Cr
4	Bank charges	85		2065	Cr
6	Sleaford Sleepers	412 ✓		1653	Cr
8	Longdendale Ltd		560 ✓	2213	Cr
10	Rent standing order	800		1413	Cr
17	Cheque no 0326	954		459	Cr
23	Electricity direct debit	68		391	Cr
28	Bank interest		32	423	Cr

Then the cash book needs updating with the items not ticked on the bank statement.

Cash book (bank columns)

Date	Details	$	Date	Details	$
20–7			20–7		
Apr 1	Balance b/d	3899	Apr 1	Bank charges	85
	Bank interest	32		Rent standing order	800
				0326 error correct	9
				Electricity direct debit	68
				Balance c/d	2969
		3931			3931
Apr 1	Balance b/d	2969			

b The items unticked on the original cash book then appear in the bank reconciliation statement:

Ebele
Bank reconciliation statement at 31 March 20–7

	$	$
Balance at bank shown in cash book		2969
Add cheques not yet presented:		
Foo Foo 0327		1113
		4082
Less amounts not yet credited:		
Tamar Valley	395	
Sales	3264	3659
Balance at bank shown on bank statement		423

2. On 30 June 20–7 the bank account of Ebele showed an overdrawn balance of $1 470 in her cash book. On the same date her bank statement showed a debit balance of $2 407.

The following differences were found:

- The bank statement showed a credit transfer of $920 from a customer, Supafood Ltd, which had not been recorded in the cash book.
- A standing order payment of $450 for rent had not yet been recorded in the cash book.
- A cheque sent to a supplier, George Chappell, for $978 did not appear on the bank statement.
- Bank charges of $85 had been omitted from the cash book.
- The bank had yet to record cash sales banked of $2 300.

a Prepare an updated cash book, balance the bank account and bring down the balance on 1 July 20–7.

b Prepare a bank reconciliation statement at 31 June 20–7.

Answer:

Cash book (bank columns)

Date	Details	$	Date	Details	$
20–7			20–7		
1 July	Supafood Ltd	920	1 July	Balance b/d	1 470
				Rent	450
				Bank charges	85
	Balance c/d	1 085			
		2 005			2 005
			1 July	Balance b/d	1 085

Ebele
Bank reconciliation statement at 31 June 20–7

	$
Balance at bank as shown in cash book	(1 085)
Add cheques not yet presented:	
George Chappell	978
	(107)
Less amounts not yet credited:	
Cash sales	2 300
Balance at bank as shown on bank statement	(2 407)

> **TIPS**
>
> Read carefully to check whether an item paid directly is coming into the business or out of it.
>
> If the balance on the cash book is a credit it is important to treat the amount as a negative figure on the bank reconciliation statement.
>
> The title for a bank reconciliation statement is at a particular date, the same as for a statement of financial position.

Progress check

1 How is a dishonoured cheque dealt with in the cash book?
2 What reasons could cause the difference between the balance of the bank according to the bank statement and the cash book?
3 State three reasons why the balance of the bank in the cash book may not match the balance of the bank on the bank statement.

Examination-style questions

1 What is true about a bank reconciliation statement? [1]

   A It is part of the double entry system.
   B It is prepared to look for errors in the cash book and the bank statement.
   C It reconciles the opening and closing bank balances.
   D It uses the totals from the sales day book.

2 The following extract was taken from Farah's cash book on 31 July 20–9.

Cash book (bank columns)

Date	Details	$	Date	Details	$
20–9			20–9		
July 1	Balance b/d	420	July 4	Schofield	402
8	J Salmon	625	9	L Turner	805
15	R Oliver	236	24	Carters	623
19	Best Fresh Ltd	982	28	Free Ways	65
29	Strangeways	354	31	Balance c/d	722
		2617			2617
Aug 1	Balance b/d	722			

14 Bank reconciliation statements

113

Farah received the following bank statement on 1 August 20–9:

Date	Details	Debit $	Credit $	Balance $	
20–9					
July 1	Balance			420	Cr
8	J Salmon		625	1 045	Cr
6	Schofield	402		643	Cr
15	R Oliver		236	879	Cr
21	Best Fresh Ltd		982	1 861	Cr
22	Bank charges	25		1 836	Cr
24	R Oliver – dishonoured	236		1 600	Cr
28	Sansa Gas	165		1 435	Cr

Farah compared the bank statement with her cash book.

a Prepare Farah's updated cash book. Balance the cash book and bring down the balance on 1 August 20–9. [5]

b Prepare the bank reconciliation statement at 31 July 20–9. [6]

3 The bank statement received by Dragon Fire Ltd shows a debit balance of $1 111 at 31 May 20–9. The accountant checks it against the cash book and makes the following discoveries:

i The bank statement shows the following items not shown in the cash book:
- a standing order for $320 paid for insurance
- a direct debit payable to Phones For All $90
- bank charges of $46
- credit transfer has been received from Best Value Company for $680.

ii The cash book has an overdrawn balance of $890 and shows the following items not shown on the bank statement:
- unpresented cheques amounting to $625
- amounts not yet credited of $1 070.

a Prepare Dragon Fire Ltd's updated cash book. Balance the cash book and bring down the balance on 1 June 20–9. [7]

b Prepare the bank reconciliation statement at 31 May 20–9. [4]

4 Complete the following table to indicate whether the item will appear in the cash book or on the bank reconciliation. If it is the cash book then complete the second column using the word debit or credit. [6]

	Cash book or bank reconciliation?	Debit or credit (for cash book entries)
Bank interest received		
Cash sales not yet credited		
Direct debit for telephone		
Standing order for rent		
Unpresented cheque		
Dishonoured cheque		

5 The bank columns of Charlene's cash book had a credit balance brought down of $890 on 1 April 20–9. The bank statement at the same date showed a debit balance of $1 505.

When Charlene compared the cash book with the bank statement she found the following:

Items on the bank statement not in the cash book:

- Bank interest received of $20.
- Credit transfer, $320, from Imran, a credit customer.
- Direct debit paid to water company, $170.
- Standing order for rent payable $780.

Items in the cashbook not on the bank statement:

- Cash sales paid in, $975.
- Cheque to Damon, a supplier, $95.

Charlene also discovered that a payment, $165 for electricity, had been entered in the cash book twice in error.

a Update the bank columns of Charlene's cash book on 1 April 20–9. Balance the cash book and bring down the balance. [7]

b Prepare the bank reconciliation at 1 April 20–9. [4]

Revision checklist

In this chapter you have learnt:

- [ ] the use and purpose of a bank statement which is the bank's version of the cash book of the business

- [ ] how to update the cash book for bank charges, bank interest paid and received, correction of errors, credit transfers, direct debits, dividends, and standing orders which have not yet been recorded in the cash book

- [ ] the purpose of a bank reconciliation statement is to match the two different viewpoints of the bank account which occur due to bank errors, uncredited deposits (debit side of the cash book) and unpresented cheques (credit side of the cash book).

Chapter 15
Journal entries and correction of errors

Learning summary

By the end of this chapter you should understand:

- the use of, and be able to process accounting data in, the book of prime entry – the general journal
- how to post the ledger entries from the general journal
- how to prepare journal entries for the provision of depreciation and to record the sale of non-current assets
- how to prepare journal entries to record accrued and prepaid expenses and accrued and prepaid incomes
- how to prepare journal entries to record irrecoverable debts and the recovery of debts written off
- how to prepare journal entries to record the creation of, and adjustments to, a provision for doubtful debts
- how to correct errors by means of journal entries
- the use of a suspense account as a temporary measure to balance the trial balance
- how to correct errors by means of suspense accounts
- how to adjust a profit or loss for an accounting period after the correction of errors
- the effect of correction of errors on a statement of financial position.

TERMS

The **general journal** or **journal** is a book of prime entry used to record transactions which cannot be recorded in any other book of prime entry.

A **suspense account** is a temporary account opened in order to make the totals of a trial balance agree.

Purpose of the general journal

The general journal is used for entries which do not fit into any of the other books of prime entry and is not part of the double entry book-keeping. A journal entry has the date of the transaction, the name of the account to be debited and the amount and the name of the account to be credited. Sometimes a narrative is also required which is a brief explanation of why the entry is being made. The transactions are then posted to the appropriate ledger accounts after the journal entry.

The items usually recorded in the general journal are:
- opening entries
- purchase and sale of non-current assets on credit
- non-regular transactions such as year-end transfers
- correction of errors.

Opening journal entries

Opening journal entries are made when the business first keeps accounting records and is simply a list of the assets owned by the business (debit column), liabilities owed by the business (credit column) and the owner's equity (also in the credit column).

Purchase and sale of non-current assets

If a non-current asset was sold for cash then it would appear in the cash book. If the transaction takes place on credit then it needs to be recorded in the general journal.

Sample question

1. Mirra's financial year ends on 30 June.

    Prepare the journal entries to record the following transactions on 1 May 20–9:

    - Purchased equipment, $2 400, on credit from Dearings Ltd.
    - Sold a motor vehicle (cost $9 900) for $6 200 to Car City Ltd.

Answer:

Mirra
Journal

Date	Details	Debit $	Credit $
20–9			
May 1	Equipment	2 400	
	Dearings Ltd		2 400
	Purchase of equipment on credit		
	Disposal of motor vehicle	9 900	
	Motor vehicle		9 900
	Car City Ltd	6 200	
	Disposal of motor vehicle		6 200
	Transfer of motor vehicle to disposal account and sale of motor vehicle on credit		
June 30	Income statement		
	Disposal of motor vehicle	3 700	
	Loss on disposal transferred to income statement		3 700

Non-regular transactions

Any other unusual item which cannot be recorded in another book of prime entry will appear in the general journal. For example, an irrecoverable debt, adjusting for prepaid or accrued expenses, transferring depreciation or creating and adjusting for a provision for doubtful debts.

The transaction is posted to the appropriate ledger accounts after the journal entry is completed. For an irrecoverable debt the general journal is debited and the trade receivable is credited. The irrecoverable debt then appears as an expense on the income statement and the trade receivables are reduced on the statement of financial position.

Sample question

2   Cleo's financial year ends on 30 June. She provided the following information for the year ended 30 June 20–9:

- Irrecoverable debts written off up to 29 June 20-9 amounted to $350.
- On 30 June 20-9 it was decided to write off as irrecoverable a debt of $100 owing by Cinder Stores and to create a provision for doubtful debts of $720.

Prepare journal entries to record these transactions and show the appropriate ledger accounts after posting these entries.

Answer:

Cleo
Journal

Date	Details	Debit $	Credit $
20–9			
June 30	Irrecoverable debts	100	
	Cinder Stores		100
	Writing off irrecoverable debts		
	Income statement	720	
	Provision for doubtful debts		720
	Creation of provision for doubtful debts		

Cleo
Sales ledger
Cinder Stores account

Date	Details	$	Date	Details	$
20–9			20–9		
June 30	Balance b/d	100	June 30	Irrecoverable debts	100
		100			100

Nominal ledger
Irrecoverable debts account

Date	Details	$	Date	Details	$
20–9			20–9		
June 29	Trade receivables written off	350	June 30	Income statement	450
30	Cinder Stores	100			
		450			450

Provision for doubtful debts account

Date	Details	$	Date	Details	$
20–9			20–9		
June 30	Balance c/d	720	June 30	Income statement	720
		720			720
			July 1	Balance b/d	720

The above account for provision for doubtful debts shows the creation of the provision. When there is an increase or decrease then it is just the change which appears on the income statement. It is recorded as an expense if the provision has increased, and as an income item added to gross profit if there has been a reduction in the provision. The closing balance (the new provision) is deducted from trade receivables on the statement of financial position.

The other non-regular transactions, adjusting for prepaid or accrued expenses and transferring depreciation, will now be explained in the following sample question.

Sample question

3   Cleo's financial year ends on 30 June. Prepare journal entries to record the following from Cleo's ledger accounts at 30 June 20–9:

- Rent, $3 300, which includes a prepayment of $480.
- Wages, $22 600, which includes an accrual of $670.
- Machinery is to be depreciated by $1 200.

Answer:

Cleo
Journal

Date	Details	Debit $	Credit $
20–9			
June 30	Income statement	2 820	
	Rent		2 820
	Transfer of rent for the year to the income statement		
	Income statement	23 270	
	Wages		23 270
	Transfer of wages for the year to the income statement		
	Income statement	1 200	
	Provision for depreciation of machinery		1 200
	Annual depreciation charge transferred to the income statement		

Correction of errors

There are six types of error that can be made which will not be revealed by the trial balance

- error of commission – wrong account of the same class
- error of complete reversal – mix up debit and credit entries
- error of omission – completely omitted from the accounting records
- error of original entry – incorrect figure when first entered in the accounting records
- error of principle – wrong class of account
- compensating errors – two or more errors cancel each other out.

If the error is not one of the six above then it will result in the totals of the trial balance not balancing. This problem can be solved temporarily by inserting a suspense account to make up the difference between the total of the debits and the credits. Once all errors have been corrected by means of a journal entry, and then in the ledger accounts, the suspense account should automatically close and there will be no closing balance. The suspense account allows financial statements to be completed before all errors have been discovered.

Sample question

4 Mirra's financial year ends on 30 June.

The totals of the trial balance prepared on 30 June 20–9 failed to agree. The difference of $170 was a shortage on the credit side. This was entered in a suspense account.

The following errors were later discovered:

i   The sales account had been under-cast by $250.

ii No entry had been made for travel expenses, $40, paid in cash.

iii A discount received for $120 had been entered as a debit to the discount allowed account.

iv A motor vehicle had been bought for $3 500 by cheque and had been debited to the bank account and credited to the motor vehicle account.

v   A credit transfer to a trade payable, Imran, for $320, had been correctly entered in the bank account, but no other entry had been made.

Prepare the necessary journal entries to correct these errors. Prepare the suspense account in Mirra's ledger.

Answer:

Mirra
General journal

Date		Details	Debit $	Credit $
20–9				
June 30		Suspense	250	
	i	Sales		250
		Sales under-cast, now corrected		
	ii	Travel expenses	40	
		Cash		40
		Omission of cash paid for travel expenses, now corrected		
	iii	Suspense	240	
		Discount allowed		120
		Discount received		120
		Discount received incorrectly debited to discount allowed, now corrected		
	iv	Motor vehicle	3 500	
		Bank		3 500
		Motor vehicle bought by cheque credited to motor vehicle and debited to bank, now corrected		
	v	Imran	320	
		Suspense		320
		Credit transfer paid to Imran entered only in the bank, now corrected		

Mirra
Nominal ledger
Suspense account

Date	Details	$	Date	Details	$
20–9			20–9		
June 30	Sales	250	June 30	Balance b/d	170
	Discount allowed	120		Imran	320
	Discount received	120			
		490			490

An entry was required in the suspense account to correct errors **i, iii** and **v** as all these affected the balancing of the trial balance.

No entry was required in the suspense account to correct errors **ii** and **iv** as these did not affect the balancing of the trial balance. Error **ii** is an error of omission and error **iv** is an error of principle.

Effect on financial statements of correcting errors

If the income statement has already been prepared prior to the errors being discovered then it will be necessary to adjust the profit figure. If the corrections are in the trading account then both gross profit and profit for the year are affected, and if the correction is made after gross profit then it is just profit for the year which will be affected. The statement of financial position will also be affected by any change in profit but also by errors concerning assets or liabilities.

Sample question

5 Mirra's financial year ends on 30 June.

The totals of the trial balance prepared on 30 June 20–9 failed to agree. The difference was entered in a suspense account and draft financial statements were prepared. The profit for the year was $16 800.

The following errors were later discovered:

i   The sales account had been under-cast by $250.

ii No entry had been made for travel expenses, $40, paid in cash.

iii A discount received for $120 had been entered as a debit to the discount allowed account.

iv A motor vehicle had been bought for $3 500 by cheque and had been debited to the bank account and credited to the motor vehicle account.

v   A credit transfer to a trade payable, Imran, for $320, had been correctly entered in the bank account, but no other entry had been made.

a   Prepare a statement to show the corrected profit for the year ended 30 June 20–9.

b   Explain if any of the errors will affect the statement of financial position at 30 June 20–9.

Answer:
a

Mirra
Statement of corrected profit for the year ended 30 June 20–9

	$
Profit for the year from income statement	16 800
Add Sales under-cast	250
Discount allowed overstated	120
Discount received understated	120
	17 290
Less Travel expenses omitted	40
Corrected profit for the year	17 250

Errors **iv** and **v** do not affect the calculation of the profit.

If the sales have been undercast, the profit will be understated and therefore $250 must be added.

If discount allowed has been overstated, the profit will be understated and so $120 must be added.

If discount received has been understated, the profit will be understated and so $120 must be added.

If travel expenses have been omitted, the profit will be overstated and therefore $40 must be deducted.

b Errors **i, ii** and **iii** do not affect items within the statement of financial position directly, but are used in the calculation of the corrected profit for the year. The profit, which is added to the capital in the statement of financial position, will be $17 250.

To correct error **iv**, the motor vehicles amount in non-current assets will need to increase by $7 000 and the bank account in the current assets section will need to decrease by $7 000.

To correct error **v**, the trade payables in the current liabilities section will need to decrease by $320.

TIPS

If a transaction does not belong in the other books of prime entry then it must be entered in the general journal.

If there is no mention of the other entry in the other account being incorrect then assume it was completed correctly.

It helps to think about the double entry of the error which has occurred already in order to decide how to solve and correct the error.

Progress check

1. State the six types of errors which will not be revealed by the trial balance.
2. Name the account which is opened when a trial balance fails to agree.
3. State three reasons to make entries in the general journal.

Examination-style questions

1. A payment for $280 travel expenses was recorded as a credit of $350 in the travel expenses account. Which entries are needed to correct this error? [1]

	Account debited	$	Account credited	$
A	Suspense	630	Travel expenses	630
B	Travel expenses	70	Suspense	70
C	Travel expenses	280	Suspense	280
D	Travel expenses	630	Suspense	630

2. The following balances remained in the books of Nehal at 31 March 20–8. She was aware that there were some book-keeping errors and that the trial balance would **not** balance.

	$
Machinery	18 700
Trade payables	3 300
Inventory	4 620
Revenue	31 500
Purchases	24 400
Cash and cash equivalents	2 100
Owner's equity	15 000
Trade receivables	2 700
Bank loan	10 000

   a Prepare the trial balance at 31 March 20–8, balancing it by the use of an appropriate account. [4]

   On inspection of her books, Nehal located the following errors:

   i A purchase of goods, $3 500, had been correctly entered in the account of a credit supplier, but had been credited to the purchases account.

   ii A credit transfer from a credit customer, $980, had been correctly entered in the customer account, but recorded in the cash and cash equivalents account as $700.

   b Prepare the general journal entries to correct errors i and ii. Narratives are **not** required. [4]

3. Shreya is a trader. Her financial year ends on 31 January. The totals of her trial balance on 31 January 20–9 did not agree. The difference was a shortage on the debit side of $140. This was entered in a suspense account.

   The following errors were later discovered:

   i Travel expenses of $130 had been credited to the travel expenses account.

   ii A purchase of machinery, $2 500, had been debited to the machinery repairs account.

   iii The sales account had been overcast by $700.

   iv The total of the discount received column in the cash book, $400, had been debited to the discount allowed account in the ledger.

v A cheque paid for electricity, $85, had been debited as $105 in the electricity account.

vi A credit transfer from B Jones, $350, had been credited to B James account.

vii Bank charges of $15 had been omitted from the books of account.

a Prepare the suspense account. Start with the balance arising from the difference on the trial balance. The account should be balanced or totalled as necessary. [6]

b Prepare journal entries to correct **two** of the errors which do **not** require correcting by means of the suspense account. Narratives are **not** required. [4]

4 Orlando prepared a trial balance but its totals did not agree. A suspense account was opened.

He later discovered the following errors:

i Rent receivable, $2 900, had been debited to the rent payable account.

ii Light and heat expenses paid, $980, had been correctly entered in the cash book, but had been recorded in the light and heat account as $890.

iii No credit entry had been made for sales on credit to Fisher, $4 200.

a Prepare the entries in the general journal to correct errors i to iii. Narratives are not required. [7]

b Prepare the suspense account showing the original difference in the trial balance. [5]

5 Dipika calculated a draft gross profit for the year ended 30 July 20–8 of $32 500. This calculation used a valuation of closing inventory of $2 400.

Dipika then discovered the following errors:

i A purchase on credit, $320, had been completely omitted from the books.

ii Closing inventory included $250 for inventory which had been damaged and now had no value, but this had not been written off.

iii The sales journal had been undercast by $300.

iv Drawings of $2 800 had been correctly entered in the cash book but credited in the capital account.

Prepare the following statement to calculate the correct gross profit for the year. Where an error has no effect on gross profit, place a tick in the 'No effect' column. [5]

Dipika

Statement of correction of gross profit for the year ended 30 July 20–8

	No effect	Increase $	Decrease $	$
Draft gross profit				32 500
Error i				
Error ii				
Error iii				
Error iv				
Corrected gross profit				

Revision checklist

In this chapter you have learnt:

- ☐ the general journal is used for transactions which do not fit into the other books of prime entry, such as provision of depreciation, sale of non-current assets, accrued and prepaid expenses and accrued and prepaid incomes

- ☐ the general journal is also used to record irrecoverable debts and the recovery of debts written off, the creation of, and adjustments to, a provision for doubtful debts

- ☐ how to correct errors by means of journal entries so that a suspense account balance can be cleared which is used as a temporary measure to balance the trial balance

- ☐ how to adjust a profit or loss for an accounting period after the correction of errors and the impact on a statement of financial position.

Control accounts

Learning summary

By the end of this chapter you should understand:

- the purposes of purchases ledger and sales ledger control accounts
- the books of prime entry as sources of information for the control account entries
- how to prepare purchase ledger and sales ledger control accounts to include credit purchases and sales, receipts and payments, cash discounts, returns, irrecoverable debts, dishonoured cheques, interest on overdue accounts, contra entries, refunds, opening and closing balances (debit and credit within each account).

TERMS

Contra entries may be referred to as inter-ledger transfers or set-offs and are when a transfer is made from an account in the sales ledger to an account of the same business/person in the purchases ledger.

A purchases ledger control account is an account summarising all the accounts of the trade payables.

A sales ledger control account is an account summarising all the accounts of the trade receivables.

Purpose and advantages of control accounts

Control accounts are also known as total accounts as they provide a summary of transactions which affect the trade receivables and trade payables. The accounts can act as a check on the individual accounts within these ledgers. It is usual for a more senior member of the accounting department to prepare the control accounts. The advantages are:

1. To reduce fraud due to a different member of the department compiling control accounts to the individual ledgers.
2. To help in locating errors if the trial balance does not balance.
3. The control accounts provide proof of the arithmetical accuracy of the ledger they control.
4. The total balances provided by the control accounts can then be used to assist in preparing draft financial statements.

Sales ledger control account

This is also known as a total trade receivables account as it contains summarised information of not just one credit customer, but all of them totalled together. The information for the sales ledger control account is taken from the books of prime entry so that it can then be checked against the total of the balances on all the individual credit customers' accounts. If the two amounts differ then further checks are needed to discover the error.

The sources of information are summarised as follows:

Item	Source of information
Sales	Sales journal
Sales returns	Sales returns journal
Receipts from credit customers	Cash book
Discounts allowed to credit customers	Cash book
Dishonoured cheques	Cash book
Refunds to credit customers	Cash book
Irrecoverable debts written off	Journal
Interest charged on overdue accounts	Journal

Sample question

1 The following information is available from the books of Sameer for July 20–8:

	$	
Sales ledger control account balance at 1 July 20–8	32 480	debit
Totals for the month		
Sales journal	36 850	
Cash sales	21 100	
Sales returns journal	1 880	
Cheques and credit transfers received from credit customers	42 650	
Discount allowed	840	
Irrecoverable debts written off	1 400	
Interest charged on overdue accounts	720	

Prepare the sales ledger control account for the month of July 20–8. Balance the account and bring down the balance on 1 August 20–8.

Answer:

Sameer
Nominal ledger
Sales ledger control account

Date	Details	$	Date	Details	$
20–8			20–8		
July 1	Balance b/d	32 480	July 31	Sales returns	1 880
31	Sales	36 850		Bank	42 650
	Interest charged	720		Discount allowed	840
				Irrecoverable debt	1 400
				Balance c/d	23 280
		70 050			70 050
Aug 1	Balance b/d	23 280			

Note that the interest charged appears on the debit side as it increases what the customers need to pay.

Purchases ledger control account

This is also known as a total trade payables account as it contains transactions concerning all of the trade payables and not just one credit supplier. Like the sales ledger control account, all of the information for the purchases ledger control account must come from the books of prime entry so that then the totals produced can be independently checked against the total of all the balances on the individual credit suppliers' accounts.

The sources of information are summarised as follows:

Item	Source of information
Purchases	Purchases journal
Purchases returns	Purchases returns journal
Payments to credit suppliers	Cash book
Discounts received from credit suppliers	Cash book
Refunds from credit suppliers	Cash book
Interest charged on overdue accounts	Journal

Sample question

2 The following information is available from the books of Sameer for July 20–8:

	$	
Purchases ledger control account balance at 1 July 20–8	21 450	credit
Totals for the month		
Purchases journal	23 540	
Cash purchases	13 100	
Purchases returns journal	2 340	
Cheques and credit transfers paid to credit suppliers	21 600	
Discount received	1 020	
Cheque refunds from credit suppliers	800	
Interest charged on overdue accounts	650	

Prepare the purchases ledger control account for the month of July 20–8. Balance the account and bring down the balance on 1 August 20–8.

Answer:

Sameer
Nominal ledger
Purchases ledger control account

Date	Details	$	Date	Details	$
20–8			20–8		
July 31	Purchases returns	2 340	July 1	Balance b/d	21 450
	Bank	21 600	31	Purchases	23 540
	Discount received	1 020		Bank (refunds)	800
	Balance c/d	21 480		Interest charged	650
		46 440			46 440
			Aug 1	Balance b/d	21 480

Balances on both sides of control accounts

Possible cause of a debit balance in a credit supplier's account	Possible cause of a credit balance in a credit customer's account
Overpayment to the supplier	Overpayment by the customer
Returning goods to the supplier after paying what was owed	Customer returning goods after paying what was owed
Paying the supplier in advance for goods	Customer paying in advance for goods
Cash discount not being deducted before payment was made	Cash discount not being deducted before payment was made

Contra entries in control accounts

Contra entries are also known as inter-ledger transfers, or set-offs, and occur when a business both sells to and buys from another business. Instead of sending what each business owes each other, the amount will be set-off so that just the excess is paid by which ever business owes the other one more. The sales ledger control account is credited with the contra amount and the purchases ledger control account is debited.

Sample question

3 The following information is available from the books of Sameer for October 20–8:

	$
Sales ledger control account balances at 1 October 20–8	29 765 debit
	625 credit
Totals for the month	
Credit sales	32 670
Cash sales	18 000
Credit notes issued to customers	970
Cheques and credit transfers received from credit customers	30 150
Discount allowed	940
Contra entry	500
Dishonoured cheque (included in cheques received)	230

Additional information:
A credit customer had made an overpayment of $250 on 31 October 20–8.

Prepare the sales ledger control account for the month of October 20–8. Balance the account and bring down the balance on 1 November 20–8.

Answer:

Sameer
Nominal ledger
Sales ledger control account

Date	Details	$	Date	Details	$
20–8			20–8		
Oct 1	Balance b/d	29 765	Oct 1	Balance b/d	625
31	Sales	32 670	31	Sales returns	970
	Bank (dishonoured)	230		Bank	30 150
				Discount allowed	940
				Contra	500
	Balance c/d	250		Balance c/d	29 730
		62 915			62 915
Nov 1	Balance b/d	29 730	Nov 1	Balance b/d	250

Note that the dishonoured cheque appears on the debit side of the control account as it is necessary to re-instate the fact that the customer still owes money.

> **TIPS**
>
> Cash sales and cash purchases do not appear in control accounts as they do not cause a trade receivable or a trade payable.
>
> Irrecoverable debts are recorded in control accounts but provision for doubtful debts are not recorded in control accounts.
>
> Entries for individual customers and suppliers are the same as for the control accounts.

Progress check

1. State two benefits of using control accounts.
2. What does the closing debit balance on a sales ledger control account represent?
3. How could a credit supplier's account have a debit balance?

Examination-style questions

1. Which item appears on the debit side of a sales ledger control account? [1]

    A discount received

    B interest charged on overdue accounts

    C irrecoverable debt

    D sales returns

2. Fred provided the following information:

	$
At 1 June 20–8:	
Trade payables	6 500
Trade receivables	8 200
For the year ended 31 May 20–9:	
Sales (all credit)	102 050
Sales returns	2 100
Purchases (all credit)	84 520
Purchases returns	1 845
Receipts from credit customers	100 305
Payments to credit suppliers	76 480
Discount allowed	1 600
Discount received	980
Irrecoverable debts	585

Additional information at 31 May 20–9:

i   Fred has paid a deposit of $500 to a trade payable for goods he will receive in July 20–9.

ii Fred owed $250 to a supplier who also owed $320 to Fred. It was agreed to offset this in the control accounts.

Prepare the sales ledger control account and the purchases ledger control account for the year. Balance the accounts and bring down the balances on 1 June 20–9. [16]

3 Amandeep provided the following information:

	$
Trade receivables at 1 January 20–9	580
During the year ended 31 December 20–9	
Receipts from credit customers	8 700
Cash sales	3 250
Invoices issued to credit customers	9 365
Credit notes issued to credit customers	280
Irrecoverable debts	145

Prepare the sales ledger control account for the year. Balance the accounts and bring down the balances on 1 January 20–0. [6]

4 Keung purchases goods on credit and maintains a purchases ledger control account. The following information is available for the month ended 31 March 20–8:

		$
20–8		
Mar 1	Amount owed to credit suppliers	42 500
31	Cheques paid to credit suppliers	64 950
	Cash purchases	2 415
	Credit purchases	84 360
	Credit notes received from credit suppliers	915
	Discount received	1 410
	Contra set off with sales ledger control account	850

Additional information:

Keung has overpaid a supplier by $130.

Prepare the purchases ledger control account for March 20–8. Balance the account and bring down the balance on 1 April 20–8. [8]

5 Complete the following table to indicate with a tick where the items would appear in a sales ledger control account. For each item name the book of prime entry from which the information would be obtained. [7]

Entry in sales ledger control account

	Debit	Credit	Source of information
Returns by credit customers			
Discount allowed			
Receipts from credit customers			
Interest charged to customer on overdue account			
Dishonoured cheque			
Irrecoverable debts written off			
Refunds to credit customers			

Revision checklist

In this chapter you have learnt:

- the purposes of purchases ledger and sales ledger control accounts to act as an independent check against the individual sales ledger and purchases ledger

- the books of prime entry are sources of information for the control account entries

- how to prepare purchase ledger and sales ledger control accounts to include credit purchases and sales, receipts and payments, cash discounts, returns, irrecoverable debts, dishonoured cheques, interest on overdue accounts, contra entries, refunds, opening and closing balances (debit and credit within each account).

Incomplete records

Chapter 17

Learning summary

By the end of this chapter you should understand:

- the disadvantages of not maintaining a full set of accounting records
- how to prepare opening and closing statements of affairs
- how to calculate profit for the year from changes in capital over time
- how to calculate sales, purchases, gross profit, trade receivables and trade payables and other figures from incomplete information
- how to prepare income statements and statements of financial position from incomplete records
- how to make adjustments to financial statements
- how to apply the techniques of mark-up, margin and inventory turnover to arrive at missing figures.

TERMS

Mark-up is the gross profit expressed as a percentage of cost price.

Margin is the gross profit expressed as a percentage of the selling price.

The rate of inventory turnover is the number of times a business replaces its inventory in a given time period.

A statement of affairs is a summary of the financial position of a business on a certain date. It is prepared instead of a statement of financial position when double entry records have not been maintained.

Reasons for incomplete records and disadvantages of not maintaining accounting records

When a small business is started, the owner is often busy establishing the business and an interest in maintaining accounting records can come at the bottom of their list of priorities. There are also circumstances where accounts are lost, stolen or damaged resulting in a lack of detail about some aspects of the business.

The disadvantages of not maintaining accounting records are:

- more expensive to prepare financial statements as the accountant will have to spend longer recreating missing records
- difficult to make decisions as unsure how successful the business is in terms of profit, cash availability, what is owed to suppliers and so on

- more difficult to borrow finance from the bank or other lenders without evidence of accounting records
- increased possibility of fraud as no controls are in place to check ledgers, for example, control accounts
- comparisons with the results of previous years and with other businesses are difficult.

Statement of affairs

A statement of affairs is a simple version of the statement of financial position based on the accounting equation:

Assets − Liabilities = Owner's equity.

You need to first calculate the opening and closing amounts of owner's equity and then you are able to compare them to discover a profit or loss, taking into account any drawings or additional equity invested. This is shown in the approach below.

Closing owner's equity

Less opening owner's equity

Add drawings

Less owner's equity introduced

= Profit for the year (loss for the year if a negative answer)

Sample question

1 Khurram is a sole trader and does not keep a full set of accounting records. He is able to provide the following information:

	1 April 20–8 $	31 March 20–9 $
Property at cost	120 000	120 000
Motor vehicles at cost	50 000	60 000
Machinery at cost	12 000	15 000
Bank	1 300	–
Bank overdraft	–	850
Cash	350	50
Trade payables	2 000	2 200
Trade receivables	3 330	3 750
Inventory	1 200	1 500

During the year ended 31 March 20–9 Khurram introduced $10 000 of his own savings. He took cash drawings of $5 000 and goods costing $2 500 for his personal use.

Calculate Khurram's profit for the year ended 31 March 20–9.

Answer:

Khurram
Calculation of profit for the year ended 31 March 20–9

	$	$
Owner's equity at 31 March 20–9		197 250
Less Owner's equity at 1 April 20–8		186 180
		11 070
Add Drawings: cash	5 000	
goods	2 500	7 500
		18 570
Less Owner's equity introduced		10 000
Profit for the year		8 570

To find the owner's equity the total liabilities are subtracted from the total assets.

Calculating sales and purchases

Cash sales and cash purchases can usually be calculated by looking at the cash book, till rolls and receipts. However, when calculating credit sales and credit purchases, trade receivables and trade payables must be taken account of in addition to payments made and received. For example, credit sales are not what the trade receivables actually pay the business, but rather the amount they should have paid taking account of starting and closing balances. Control accounts or totals accounts can be used to calculate missing information.

Sample question

2 Anisa is a sole trader who maintains a bank account but not a full set of accounting records. She provided the following information:

	1 May 20–8 $	30 April 20–9 $
Trade receivables	62 000	74 500
Trade payables	25 000	39 100

During the year ended 30 April 20–9 receipts from credit customers totalled $224 500 (after the deduction of $3 800 cash discount). $103 800 was paid to credit suppliers (after the deduction of $5 250 cash discount).

Calculate the credit sales and credit purchases for the year ended 30 April 20–9.

Answer:

Total trade receivables account

Date	Details	$	Date	Details	$
20–8			20–9		
May 1	Balance b/d	62 000	Apr 30	Bank	224 500
20–9				Discount allowed	3 800
Apr 30	Sales	240 800		Balance c/d	74 500
		302 800			302 800
May 1	Balance b/d	74 500			

Total trade payables account

Date	Details	$	Date	Details	$
20–9			20–8		
Apr 30	Bank	103 800	May 1	Balance b/d	25 000
	Discount received	5 250	20–9		
	Balance c/d	39 100	Apr 30	Purchases	123 150
		148 150			148 150
			May 1	Balance b/d	39 100

The sales and purchases figures calculated above are the missing figures in the calculations and will be added to any cash sales and cash purchases. They will appear in the trading account section of the income statement. The discount allowed and discount received will also appear in the income statement.

Mark-up, margin and inventory turnover

Many businesses, especially sole traders, use a simple system of adding a set percentage mark-up to their goods or services so that they know they are making a profit margin on everything they sell. We can use this information to calculate sales or the cost of sales if these figures are not supplied. The important distinction is that with margin the gross profit is measured as a percentage of selling price, and with mark-up the gross profit is measured as a percentage of the cost price.

Sometimes the rate of inventory turnover can be used to calculate an unknown figure in the trading account section of the income statement. The formula is:

$$\frac{\text{Cost of sales}}{\text{Average inventory}}$$

The average inventory is the opening inventory plus closing inventory divided by two.

Sample question

3 Anisa is a trader. The financial year ends on 30 November. The following information is provided:

Inventory 1 December 20–7	$50 000
Inventory 30 November 20–8	$55 000
Mark-up on cost	20%
Rate of inventory turnover	8 times

Calculate, by means of the trading account section of an income statement, the purchases for the year ended 30 November 20–8.

Answer:

Anisa
Income statement for the year ended 30 November 20–8

	$	$
Revenue		504 000
Less Cost of sales		
Opening inventory	50 000	
Purchases	425 000	
	475 000	
Less Closing inventory	55 000	420 000
Gross profit		84 000

- An outline of the statement was prepared and the figures for opening and closing inventory were inserted, with gaps left for revenue, purchases, cost of sales and gross profit.

  The average inventory was calculated as $\dfrac{\text{Opening inventory} + \text{Closing inventory}}{2}$.

  $\dfrac{50\,000 + 55\,000}{2} = \$52\,500$

- The cost of sales was calculated as rate of inventory turnover = $\dfrac{\text{Cost of sales}}{\text{Average inventory}}$.

  $\dfrac{\text{Cost of sales}}{52\,500} = 8$ so, cost of sales = $420 000.

- The cost of sales can then be inserted and the missing purchases figure can be found.

- Finally, gross profit can be calculated by finding 20% of the cost of sales and this is added to the cost of sales to calculate the revenue.

Stages in completing financial statements from incomplete records

The approach will vary according to the information given. Your role is to act as a detective and sort out what amounts you definitely know and what needs to be calculated.

1 If you do know the assets and liabilities at the start or end of the year then you can complete a statement of affairs in order to calculate the opening and/or closing owner's equity.

2 Use total payables accounts to calculate credit purchases and total receivables accounts to calculate credit sales. Cash sales and cash purchases can often be found in the cash book.

3 Use mark-up, margin or rate of inventory turnover as appropriate remembering that mark-up is based on cost of sales and margin is based on sales.

4 Draw up the outline of the financial statements and include as much information as you can find remembering to take account of other payables and other receivables. It is the amount that should have been paid, rather than what was actually paid, which needs to be included in expenses.

> **TIPS**
>
> Set out the layout of whichever statement you are asked to complete and then fill in the missing gaps.
>
> Margin is linked to sales and mark-up to cost of sales.
>
> Incomplete records brings together a range of skills such as double entry, control accounts, ratio analysis, completing financial statements and making adjustments so these areas need to be practiced alongside this topic area.

Progress check

1 How can credit sales be calculated?
2 State two advantages of maintaining double entry book-keeping.
3 Why don't cash purchases appear in the total payables account?

Examination-style questions

1 Ricardo did not maintain a full set of accounting records. He was able to provide the following information:

	$
Trade payables at 1 September 20–8	890
During the year ended 31 August 20–9	
Payments to credit suppliers	5 640
Invoices received	6 230
Credit notes received from credit suppliers	185
Trade payables at 31 August 20–9	995

Prepare the total trade payables account for the year ended 31 August 20–9 to determine the discount received by Ricardo during the year.

[6]

2   Max is a sole trader and provides the following information for the year ended 31 January 20–9:

Revenue	$900 000
Gross profit margin	25%
Rate of inventory turnover	15 times
Inventory at 1 February 20–8	$40 000

Prepare the trading account section of the income statement for the year ended 31 January 20–9. [6]

3   Kiyoko did not maintain a full set of accounting records and provided the following information:

i   At 1 March 20–8, the non-current assets which originally cost $8 200 had accumulated depreciation of $3 500. Kiyoko's policy is to depreciate non-current assets at 15% per annum using the reducing balance method.

ii   Kiyoko's capital on 1 March 20–8 was $6 200. During the year she made drawings of $3 050.

iii   On 28 February 20–9:

	$
Inventory	820
Other operating expenses accrued	230
Bank overdraft	415
Trade receivables	620
Trade payables	745

Prepare Kiyoko's statement of financial position at 28 February 20–9. Give both opening and closing balances in the capital section. Insert profit for the year as a balancing figure. [10]

4   A trader provided the following information at the end of the first year of trading:

	$
Closing inventory	950
Profit for the year	2 500
Purchases	4 600
Revenue	8 200

What were the expenses for the year? [1]

A $2 050   B $3 600   C $3 650   D $4 550

5   Vicky Hoang has not kept adequate records for her business for the year ended 30 June 20–7. She has supplied the following information:

Mark-up on cost	25%
Amount paid to trade payables	$363 000
Business expenses (excluding depreciation)	$52 100
Drawings	$20 500

	30 June 20–6 $	30 June 20–7 $
Delivery van	12 000	10 000
Cash and cash equivalents	3 300	12 075
Trade payables	8 000	6 500
Inventory	6 000	12 000
Prepaid business expenses	220	450

a   Prepare the income statement for Vicky Hoang for the year ended 30 June 20–7. [8]

b   Prepare a statement of financial position at 30 June 20–7. [8]

Revision checklist

In this chapter you have learnt:

- the disadvantages of not maintaining a full set of accounting records
- how to prepare opening and closing statements of affairs in order to calculate profit for the year from changes in capital over time
- how to calculate sales, purchases, gross profit, trade receivables and trade payables and other figures from incomplete information
- how to prepare income statements and statements of financial position from incomplete records and how to make adjustments to financial statements
- how to apply the techniques of mark-up, margin and inventory turnover to arrive at missing figures.

Accounts of clubs and societies

Learning summary

By the end of this chapter you should understand:

- how to distinguish between receipts and payments accounts and income and expenditure accounts
- how to prepare receipts and payments accounts
- how to prepare accounts for revenue-generating activities, e.g. refreshments and subscriptions
- how to prepare income and expenditure accounts and statements of financial position
- how to make adjustments to financial statements, define and calculate the accumulated fund.

TERMS

The **accumulated fund** consists of the surpluses (less any deficits) which have accumulated over the life of the organisation. It replaces owner's equity in the statement of financial position of a club or society.

A **deficit** arises when the expenses of a non-trading organisation exceed the gains.

An **income and expenditure account** is prepared annually by a non-trading organisation. It compares the gains and the expenses to calculate the surplus or deficit.

A **non-trading organisation** is an organisation formed to provide facilities and services for members. They are not formed with the aim of making a profit.

A **receipts and payments account** is a summary of the cash book which is prepared annually by a non-trading organisation.

Subscriptions are amounts members of an organisation pay, usually annually, to use the facilities provided by the club or society.

A **surplus** arises when the gains of a non-trading organisation exceed the expenses.

Accounting for non-trading organisations

Clubs and societies are not set up with the aim to make profits; they are non-profit making organisations such as sports clubs and amateur dramatic groups. It is still important that accounting records are kept in order to make decisions, such as an appropriate rate for subscriptions. Subscriptions are often the main source of income and represent the amounts members pay to use the facilities.

A treasurer is appointed to be responsible for collecting money due and paying out money owed. They will then compile financial statements at the end of the financial year which normally consist of a receipts and payments account (summary of the cash book), a trading account section of an income statement (if they have a shop or café), an income and expenditure account (income statement) and a statement of financial position.

Receipts and payments account

This statement is the equivalent of a simple cash book. It is a summary of all the receipts and payments of the club for the year. Its purpose is to show the club's members where the cash has come from and where it has gone to and the balance in hand at the year-end.

It does not show the members:

1. adjustments for accruals and prepayments
2. the assets owned by the club and depreciation
3. any liabilities that are owed.

Sample question

1. Millbrook Cricket Club was formed to encourage all ages to play and enjoy cricket. It also has a shop where members can purchase sportswear.

    On 1 November 20–8 the club had $3 800 in the bank. The treasurer provided the following list of receipts and payments for the year ended 31 October 20–9:

	$
Subscriptions received	21 250
Receipts from shop sales	7 480
Purchases of goods for resale	6 200
Wages – shop assistant	1 350
cricket coach	7 460
Rent	5 150
General expenses	3 800
Purchase of new cricket equipment	4 500

    All receipts are paid into the bank and all payments are made by cheque or credit transfer.

    Prepare the receipts and payments account of Millbrook Cricket Club for the year ended 31 October 20–9.

Answer:

Millbrook Cricket Club
Receipts and payments account for the year ended 31 October 20–9

	Receipts	$		Payments	$
20–8			20–9		
Nov 1	Balance b/d	3 800	Oct 31	Rent of grounds	5 150
20–9				Purchases	6 200
Oct 31	Subscriptions	21 250		Wages – shop	1 350
	Shop sales	7 480		Wages – club	7 460
				Cricket equipment	4 500
				Club expenses	3 800
				Balance c/d	4 070
		32 530			32 530
Nov 1	Balance b/d	4 070			

Trading sections of income statements and income and expenditure accounts

It is possible that the club or society may run profit-making enterprises as part of their operation. The usual item here is that many clubs or societies have a club house or hall where they have a shop or café. These will be run on a profit-making basis. If this is the case, a trading account section is compiled for the shop or café, and any profit or loss is added into the income and expenditure account as income, for example profit on shop, or if there is a loss, as an expense.

In an income and expenditure account the top half of the account records income and the bottom expenditure. The key here is that clubs and societies can receive income from all sorts of different areas such as subscriptions, donations and fundraising activities. If fundraising activities involve any expenses such as prizes, then this amount needs to be set off against the income to produce the overall income received. The expenditure section is exactly the same as expenses on an income statement. We record all the expenses associated with running the club here including depreciation and adjustments for accrued expenses and prepayments. If any members will not be paying the subscriptions they owe, then this is an irrecoverable debt and is listed in the expenses section. Income less expenditure then generates either a surplus or a deficit figure (not profit or loss) that is then carried forward to the statement of financial position.

Sample question

2 Millbrook Cricket Club was formed to encourage all ages to play and enjoy cricket. It also has a shop where members can purchase sportswear.

Its receipts and payments account for the year ended 31 October 20–9 is as follows:

Millbrook Cricket Club
Receipts and payments account for the year ended 31 October 20–9

	Receipts	$		Payments	$
20–8			20–9		
Nov 1	Balance b/d	3 800	Oct 31	Rent of grounds	5 150
20–9				Purchases	6 200
Oct 31	Subscriptions	21 250		Wages – shop	1 350
	Shop sales	7 480		Wages – club	7 460
				Cricket equipment	4 500
				Club expenses	3 800
				Balance c/d	4 070
		32 530			32 530
Nov 1	Balance b/d	4 070			

Other information is as follows:

	1 November 20–8 $	31 October 20–9 $
Subscriptions in advance	820	600
Cricket equipment at valuation	10 500	12 400
Shop inventory	920	865
Amounts owed to shop suppliers	210	195

a Prepare the shop income statement for the year ended 31 October 20–9.

b Prepare the club's income and expenditure account for the year ended 31 October 20–9.

Answer:

a

Millbrook Cricket Club
Income statement for shop for the year ended 31 October 20–9

	$	$
Sales		7 480
Opening inventory	920	
Purchases (6 200 – 210 + 195)	6 185	
Closing inventory	865	
Cost of sales		6 240
Gross profit		1 240
Shop wages		1 350
Loss for the year		(110)

Note that the purchases need adjusting for the amounts owed to the supplier at the start and end of the year. Last year's amount owed is subtracted and this year's is added.

b

Millbrook Cricket Club
Income and expenditure account for the year ended 31 October 20–9

	$	$
Income		
Subscriptions (21 250 + 820 – 600)		21 470
Expenditure		
Depreciation cricket equipment	2 600	
Rent of grounds	5 150	
Club wages	7 460	
Loss of shop	110	
Club expenses	3 800	19 120
Surplus for the year		2 350

The subscriptions have been adjusted to show what should have been paid, not the actual amount paid. In this case the $820 paid in advance needs adding to the subscriptions received of $21 250, and then subtract the subscriptions received in advance for the following year of $600. Note that the loss of shop is included in the expenses. If a profit had been made it would appear in the income section and be added to the subscriptions.

Statement of financial position

This is prepared in a similar way to any other business. The net resources of the club or society are financed by the accumulated funds in place of owner's equity. Any surplus from the income and expenditure account is added to the fund and any deficit is subtracted. Members are not entitled to take drawings as they are not the owners.

Sample question

3 Millbrook Cricket Club was formed to encourage all ages to play and enjoy cricket. It also has a shop where members can purchase sportswear.

On 1 November 20–8 the following balances appeared in the books of the Club:

	$
Property at cost	24 700
Cricket equipment at cost	13 700
Provision for depreciation of cricket equipment	3 200
Balance at bank	3 800
Shop inventory	920
Trade payables	210
Subscriptions in advance	820
Accumulated fund	38 890

The income and expenditure account for the year ended 31 October 20–9 showed a surplus of $2 350. During the year ended 31 October 20–9 new cricket equipment costing $4 500 was purchased. The depreciation on the cricket equipment for the year amounted to $2 600.

On 31 October 20–9:

	$
Balance at bank	4 070
Shop inventory	865
Trade payables	195
Subscriptions paid in advance by members	600

Prepare the statement of financial position of Millbrook Cricket Club at 31 October 20–9.

Answer:

Millbrook Cricket Club
Statement of financial position at 31 October 20–9

	Cost $	Accumulated depreciation $	Net book value $
Non-current assets			
Property	24 700	–	24 700
Cricket equipment	18 200	5 800	12 400
	42 900	5 800	37 100
Current assets			
Shop inventory			865
Bank		4 070	
		4 935	
Total assets			42 035
Accumulated funds and liabilities			
Accumulated fund			
Opening balance			38 890
Plus Surplus for the year			2 350
			41 240
Current liabilities			
Trade payables			195
Subscriptions prepaid			600
			795
Total liabilities			42 035

Note that if there were subscriptions owing then these would appear in the current assets section as the money is owed by members. The starting amount for the accumulated fund was found by adding the assets at 1 November 20–8 and subtracting the liabilities (the accounting equation).

Subscriptions

Annual membership subscriptions of clubs and societies are usually payable one year in advance. This means that a club or society receives payments from members for benefits they have yet to enjoy. Therefore, payments made by members in advance will be shown on the statement of financial position as a current liability and those members who still owe subscriptions at the financial year-end are a current asset.

Sample question

4 Mossley Amateur Dramatic Society had membership subscriptions paid in advance of $1 600 and subscriptions owing of $250 on 1 April 20–8.

During the year ended 31 March 20–9 the society received receipts of subscriptions paid into the bank of $19 200. At 31 March 20–9 subscriptions in advance amounted to $1 850 and subscriptions outstanding of $300.

Prepare the subscriptions account in the books of Mossley Amateur Dramatic Society for the year ended 31 March 20–9.

Answer:

Mossley Amateur Dramatic Society
Subscriptions account

Date	Details	$	Date	Details	$
20–8			20–8		
Apr 1	Balance b/d	250	Apr 1	Balance b/d	1 600
20–9			20–9		
Mar 31	Income and expenditure	19 000	Mar 31	Bank	19 200
	Balance c/d	1 850		Balance c/d	300
		21 100			21 100
Apr 1	Balance b/d	300	Apr 1	Balance b/d	1 850

TIPS

If a club or society has a profit-generating aspect to it, ensure that all relevant costs are attached to calculating the profit and make adjustments for any trade payables.

The subscription amount which appears on the income and expenditure account is that amount that should have been received and not the actual amount entered into the receipts and payments account.

Progress check

1 What is the owner's equity called for a club or society?
2 Why is the term surplus used rather than profit in the income and expenditure account?
3 Where do subscriptions paid in advance appear in the statement of financial position?

Examination-style questions

1. The activities of the Heathcliff Hockey Club include the running of a sports clothing shop. On 1 January the accumulated fund of the club amounted to $17 400 and on 31 December $19 100.

   What does this increase mean? [1]

   A The non-current assets increased by $1 700.

   B There was an income from the shop of $1 700.

   C There was a surplus for the year of $1 700.

   D The subscriptions owed by members are $1 700.

2. The treasurer of Staley Chess Club provided the following information:

Balances on 1 November 20–8:	
Subscriptions outstanding	$320
Subscriptions prepaid	$480
Subscriptions received and banked during the year $9 200	
None of the subscriptions outstanding at 1 November 20–8 were received. These were written off as irrecoverable.	
Balances on 31 October 20–9:	
Subscriptions outstanding	$185
Subscriptions prepaid	$390

   Prepare the subscriptions account for the year ended 31 October 20–9. Balance the account and bring down the balances on 1 November 20–9. [7]

3. Ambleside Climbing Society have provided the following balances at 30 April 20–7 after preparing the income and expenditure account:

	$
Subscriptions prepaid	520
Subscriptions outstanding	365
First Aider's salary owing	260
Inventory of ropes	1 600
Surplus	420
Insurance prepaid	145
Equipment at valuation	6 500
6% bank loan (repayable 31 January 20–9)	2 000
Bank	695 debit
Trade payables	235

   Prepare the statement of financial position at 30 April 20–7 showing the value of the accumulated fund at 1 May 20–6 and 30 April 20–7.

4 Ashton Football Club is an amateur rugby club and also runs a café for members. It provided the following information:

At 31 July 20–7:

	$
Bank balance – debit	8 200
Subscriptions in advance	300
Amount due to suppliers for café	420
Inventory of café	965
Sports equipment at valuation	4 200

During the year ended 31 July 20–8:

Subscriptions received	12 620
Receipts from café	5 650
Payments to suppliers for café	4 500
Payment for purchases of new sports equipment	4 630
Rent paid for sports ground	3 600
Wages of football coach paid	2 820
Other operating expenses paid	1 935

At 31 July 20–8:

	$
Subscriptions owed	220
Amount due to suppliers for café	385
Inventory of café	840
Sports equipment at valuation	6 830

a Prepare the receipts and payments account for the year ended 31 July 20–8. [6]

b Prepare the subscriptions account for the year ended 31 July 20–8. Bring down the balance on 1 August 20–8. [5]

c Calculate the café profit for the year ended 31 July 20–8. [6]

d Prepare the income and expenditure account for the year ended 31 July 20–8. [8]

e Prepare the statement of financial position at 31 July 20–8. [9]

Revision checklist

In this chapter you have learnt:

- ☐ receipts and payments accounts are a simple cash book and income and expenditure accounts are similar to income statements

- ☐ how to prepare accounts for revenue-generating activities, e.g. refreshments using a trading account, and subscriptions, allowing for subscriptions paid in advance and owing at the end of the financial year

- ☐ how to prepare income and expenditure accounts and statements of financial position

- ☐ how to make adjustments to financial statements

- ☐ how to calculate the accumulated fund using the accounting equation.

Chapter 19

Partnerships

Learning summary

By the end of this chapter you should understand:

- the advantages and disadvantages of forming a partnership
- the importance and contents of a partnership agreement
- the purpose of an appropriation account
- how to prepare income statements, appropriation accounts and statements of financial position
- how to record interest on partners' loans, interest on capital, interest on drawings, partners' salaries and the division of the balance of profit or loss
- how to make adjustments to financial statements
- the uses of, and differences between, capital and current accounts
- how to draw up partners' capital and current accounts in ledger account form and as part of a statement of financial position.

TERMS

A **partnership** is a business in which two or more people work together as owners with a view to making profits.

A **partnership agreement** is a document setting out the rules under which the partners will operate the business, including profit-sharing arrangements.

A partnership **appropriation account** is part of the year-end financial statements. It shows the division of the profit or loss between the partners.

The **residual profit** is the profit remaining after adjusting the profit for the year for interest on drawings, interest on capital and partners' salaries. It is divided between the partners in the agreed profit-sharing ratio.

Introduction to partnerships

The Partnership Act 1890 defines partnership as 'the relationship which subsists between persons carrying on business with a view to a profit'. Partnerships, like sole traders, still have unlimited liability, so you have to trust your partners or you could be faced with losing your personal assets if the partnership fails. The decisions made by one partner are legally binding on the others and this is known as joint and several liability. A partnership may be formed because there is too much work for a sole trader or because the sole trader wants to be able to expand and needs finance and expertise from elsewhere.

Advantages and disadvantages of partnerships

Advantages	Disadvantages
Additional capital introduced	Unlimited liability
Can share the workload and specialise	Potential disagreements
Variety of ideas and solutions to problems	Share profits
Cover for holidays or sickness	Decisions may take longer to put into place
Share risks	May be hard to reach agreement due to different opinions
	All partners are responsible for the debts of the business

> **TIPS**
>
> If you are asked about advantages and disadvantages of becoming a partnership for an existing sole trader, it is important not to use responses which apply to a sole trader as well, such as unlimited liability.
>
> Loans from partners are not part of the capital of the business and are treated in the same way as any other loan. The interest on the loan is an expense on the income statement and not an appropriation of profit.

Partnership agreements

It is usual for a partnership to draw up a written agreement. such as a deed of partnership, which sets out the terms and financial agreements. This avoids disagreements at a later stage.

Likely contents of a partnership agreement includes the following:

- Capital introduced – how much each partner is required to contribute to the business.

- Profit/loss sharing ratio – this is how the partners share the profits or losses and can be done according to who works the most hours, who is the most skilled, who contributed most capital, etc.

- Interest on capital – this is interest paid to the partners according to how much capital they have invested. The more they have invested, the more interest they receive. This reduces the amount of profit in the partnership but improves the individual partner's current account.

- Partnership salaries – it may be agreed that some partners receive a salary in addition to their share of profit. This could be to ensure a partner receives a minimum income.

- Drawings and interest on drawings – drawings are the amounts that the partners withdraw from the partnership. Interest may be charged in order to discourage excessive drawings. A serious cash shortage could be caused if partners withdraw significant amounts of cash.

- Interest on loans – a partner may wish to lend the partnership finance as this may incur less interest than borrowing from a financial institution such as a bank.

Purpose of an appropriation account

Income statements are exactly the same for partnerships as they are for a sole trader. The only difference comes after the profit for the year has been calculated. An appropriation account is now added on to show how the profit or loss for the year is distributed amongst the partners. There are just four possible entries that may occur: interest on drawings, interest on capital, salaries and then the share of the profit or loss. Adjustments are made from the point of view of the partnership and not of the individual partner. Interest on capital and interest on drawings are calculated for each partner separately and labelled. Any partnership salary also needs labelling to show which partner will receive the salary. The appropriation account then provides amounts which need entering into the current accounts of the partners.

Sample question

1 Arun and Deepro are in partnership. Their financial year ends on 31 July. They provide the following information:

		$
Capital on 1 August 20–7	Arun	55 000
	Deepro	60 000
Drawings for the year ended 31 July 20–8	Arun	9 000
	Deepro	6 500
Profit for the year ended 31 July 20–8		30 500

The partnership agreement includes the following terms:
- Interest on capital is allowed at 6% per annum.
- Interest on drawings is charged at 4% per annum.
- Arun is entitled to a partnership salary of $12 000 per annum.
- Residual profits are to be shared equally.

Prepare the profit and loss appropriation account for the year ended 31 July 20–8.

Answer:

Arun and Deepro
Profit and loss appropriation account for the year ended 31 July 20–8

		$	$
Profit for the year			30 500
Add Interest on drawings	Arun	360	
	Deepro	260	620
			31 120
Less Interest on capital	Arun	3 300	
	Deepro	3 600	6 900
			24 220
Less Partner's salary	Arun		12 000
			12 220
Profit share	Arun	6 110	
	Deepro	6 110	12 220

Partners' ledger accounts

Capital accounts are kept in order to keep track of the amounts invested by each partner and are sometimes known as fixed capital accounts. Keeping a separate capital account allows interest on capital to be easily calculated. The credit balance on the capital account indicates that the business owes this amount to the partner.

Current accounts are used to show all other movements involving the partners other than changes to the capital account. It is preferable to have a credit balance on the current account as this indicates that the business owes the partner, whereas a debit balance means the partner owes the business and has removed more than they were entitled to.

Sample question

2 Arun and Deepro are in partnership. Their financial year ends on 31 July. They provide the following information:

	Arun $	Deepro $
On 1 August 20–7:		
Capital account	55 000	60 000
Current account	2 200 credit	1 500 debit
For the year ended 31 July 20–8:		
Drawings	9 000	6 500
Interest on drawings	360	260
Interest on capital	3 300	3 600
Partner's salary	12 000	–
Profit share	6 110	6 110

Prepare the capital accounts and the current accounts of Arun and Deepro for the year ended 31 July 20–8.

Answer:

Arun and Deepro
Capital accounts

Date	Details	Arun $	Deepro $	Date	Details	Arun $	Deepro $
				20–7			
				1 Aug	Bal b/d	55 000	60 000

Arun and Deepro
Current accounts

Date	Details	Arun $	Deepro $	Date	Details	Arun $	Deepro $
20–7				20–7			
1 Aug	Bal b/d		1 500	1 Aug	Bal b/d	2 200	
20–8				20–8			
31 Jul	Drawings	9 000	6 500	31 Jul	Interest on capital	3 300	3 600
	Interest on drawings	360	260		Salary	12 000	
	Bal c/d	14 250	1 450		Profit share	6 110	6 110
		23 610	9 710			23 610	9 710
				1 Aug	Bal b/d	14 250	1 450

Statements of financial position for a partnership

A statement of financial position is the same layout as for the sole trader but instead of having the owner's equity = profit for the year – drawings, the partners' capital and current accounts are shown as below.

Arun and Deepro
Extract from statement of financial position at 31 July 20–8

	Arun $	Deepro $	Total $
Capital accounts	55 000	60 000	115 000
Current accounts	14 250	1 450	15 700
	69 250	61 450	130 700

If Deepro had continued to have a debit balance then his current account would appear as a minus.

Progress check

1. What advantages could a sole trader gain by entering into a partnership?
2. State three entries which could appear in a partner's current account.
3. Why would a partnership reward its partners with interest on capital?

Examination-style questions

1. On 1 January 20–8 Kathryn had a credit balance on her current account of $3 500. During the year the following were recorded in her current account:

	$
Interest on capital	4 200
Interest on drawings	376
Share of residual loss	5 500
Drawings	8 800

   What was the balance on Kathryn's current account on 1 January 20–9? [1]

   A $6 224 debit
   B $6 976 debit
   C $13 976 debit
   D $14 624 debit

2. Mittzy, Sue and Karl own a sports equipment shop. They share profits and losses in the ratios of 2:2:1 respectively and have provided you with the following information for the year ended 30 September 20–9:

	Mittzy $	Sue $	Karl $
Capital	78 000	42 000	95 500
Partner's salary	10 000	0	15 000
Drawings	4 000	2 500	3 300

   Interest on drawings is 5% per annum and interest on capital is 6% per annum. The profit for the year was $64 800.

   Prepare an appropriation account for the year ended 30 September 20–9. [7]

3. Hiroshi and Mitsu had been sole traders for several years and then decided to form a partnership on 1 March 20–9 combining their assets and liabilities.

	Hiroshi $	Mitsu $
Assets		
Property	25 000	
Motor vehicle	9 500	
Machinery		16 800
Inventory	4 200	2 800
Trade receivables	4 350	
Cash and cash equivalents	5 850	
Liabilities		
Trade payables	3 400	1 850
Bank overdraft		2 450

   a Calculate the opening capital of each partner. [2]

   b Prepare the statement of financial position of the new partnership at 1 March 20–9. [6]

4. Anthony and Beatrix are in partnership. Their partnership agreement states that interest on capital is paid at a rate of 15% per annum and that their profits and losses are shared in the ratio of 3:1 respectively.

   The following information is available:

	$	
At 1 September 20–8:		
Capital accounts		
Anthony	70 000	
Beatrix	40 000	
Current accounts		
Anthony	1 800	debit
Beatrix	4 300	credit
For the year ended 31 August 20–9:		
Profit for the year	58 000	
Drawings		
Anthony	28 500	
Beatrix	19 800	

On 1 February 20–9 Beatrix introduced additional capital of $20 000 into the partnership by cheque.

a Prepare the appropriation account for the year ended 31 August 20–9. [4]

b Prepare the capital accounts for the year ended 31 August 20–9 and balance the accounts and bring down the balances. [4]

c Prepare the current accounts for the year ended 31 August 20–9 and balance the accounts and bring down the balances. [7]

5 Arthur and Charlotte are in partnership sharing profits and losses in the ratio 3:2. Interest is allowed on capital at the rate of 6% per annum and is charged on drawings at 10%. A salary is paid to Charlotte of $9 400 per annum.

The following balances were extracted from the books on 31 December 20–9:

	$	
Property at cost	382 945	
Motor vehicles at cost	50 000	
Fixtures and fittings at cost	22 500	
Provision for depreciation for motor vehicles	18 000	
Provision for depreciation for fixtures and fittings	4 500	
Capital accounts:		
Arthur	80 000	
Charlotte	60 000	
Current accounts:		
Arthur	1 500	credit
Charlotte	9 800	debit
Drawings:		
Arthur	4 000	
Charlotte	6 000	
7% bank loan repayable in five years	15 000	
Bank loan interest paid	525	
Trade receivables	32 800	
Trade payables	43 500	
Cash and cash equivalents	2 200	
Provision for doubtful debts	1 200	

	$
Revenue	680 000
Inventory at 1 January 20–9	28 500
Purchases	320 000
Sales returns	2 000
Purchases returns	3 200
Wages and salaries	26 400
Electricity and water	1 500
Insurance	2 300
Motor vehicle expenses	1 750
General expenses	22 500

Additional information:

- Inventory at 31 December 20–9 was valued at $31 000.
- At 31 December, wages and salaries of $400 were owing and insurance of $250 had been prepaid.
- Fixtures and fittings costing $3 000, and with an accumulate depreciation of $600, had been sold for $2 600. A cheque was received on 26 December 20–9. No entries had been recorded in the books.
- Depreciation is to be charged on all non–current assets owned at the end of each year with the exception of property.

  Motor vehicles are depreciated at the rate of 20% per annum using the reducing balance method.

  Office fixtures are depreciated at the rate of 10% per annum using the straight line method.
- Trade receivables include a debt of $2 800 which is irrecoverable. The provision for doubtful debts is to be 5% of the remaining trade receivables.

a Prepare the income statement and appropriation account for the year ended 31 December 20–9. [19]

b Prepare the current accounts for the year ended 31 December 20–9. Balance the accounts and bring down the balances on 1 January 20–0. [8]

c Prepare the statement of financial position at 31 December 20–9. [11]

Revision checklist

In this chapter you have learnt:

- [ ] the advantages and disadvantages of forming a partnership
- [ ] the importance and contents of a partnership agreement in case of later disagreements
- [ ] the purpose of an appropriation account to share the profit between the partners
- [ ] how to prepare income statements, appropriation accounts and statements of financial position
- [ ] how to record interest on partners' loans (in expense section of the income statement), interest on capital, interest on drawings, partners' salaries and the division of the balance of profit or loss
- [ ] how to make adjustments to financial statements
- [ ] the uses of, and differences between, capital (permanent changes) and current accounts (all other movements)
- [ ] how to draw up partners' capital and current accounts in ledger account form and as part of a statement of financial position.

Chapter 20

Manufacturing accounts

Learning summary

By the end of this chapter you should understand:

- how to distinguish between direct and indirect costs, direct material, direct labour, prime cost and factory overheads
- how to make adjustments for work in progress
- how to calculate factory cost of production
- how to prepare manufacturing accounts: income statements and statements of financial position
- how to make adjustments to financial statements.

TERMS

Cost of production is prime cost plus factory overheads, adjusted for any work in progress at the start and at the end of the year. It is the total cost of manufacturing the goods completed.

A **manufacturing account** is part of the annual financial statements and is used to calculate the cost of goods produced.

Prime cost is the total of the direct materials, direct labour and direct expenses. It is the cost of the essentials necessary for production.

Work in progress is the goods which are partly completed at the end of the financial year.

Purpose of a manufacturing account

A retailer buys and sells completed products, whereas a manufacturer has to produce the products to sell. A manufacturing account is prepared to show all the costs associated with the making of these products within the factory. A manufacturing account is split into two sections:

1. The prime cost section, which calculates the total of the direct manufacturing cost of the products, and the direct costs, which include raw materials, direct labour (workers who are actively involved in making and packaging products) and direct expenses such as royalties (for example, a payment to the original inventor of a product).

2. The manufacturing overheads section, which identifies all the other costs (indirect costs) associated with the production of the products, for example factory rent, machine maintenance and machine depreciation. This section needs adding to the prime cost section to calculate the cost of production.

> **TIPS**
>
> Ensure that the manufacturing account only includes information about the factory and actual manufacturing process and not other non-production costs such as administration, finance or distribution costs.
>
> Use the correct labels within the manufacturing account, particularly for cost of raw materials consumed, prime cost and cost of production.
>
> Remember to add the overheads within the manufacturing account as a common mistake is to subtract them from the prime cost.

Sample questions

1 Identify which of the following costs are either direct or indirect manufacturing costs.

Cost	Direct	Indirect
Cost of raw materials		
Factory supervisor salary		
Rent of factory		
Machinery depreciation		
Royalties		

Answer:

Cost	Direct	Indirect
Cost of raw materials	✓	
Factory supervisor salary		✓
Rent of factory		✓
Machinery depreciation	✓	
Royalties	✓	

2 The following information is available for Sugden Ltd for the year ended 31 January 20–9:

	$
Direct wages	21 000
Factory insurance	3 800
Inventory of raw materials at 1 February 20–8	58 500
Inventory of raw materials at 31 January 20–9	63 400
Factory rent	19 900
Purchases of raw materials	240 800
Royalties	3 500

Prepare the prime cost section of the manufacturing account for Sugden Ltd for the year ended 31 January 20–9.

Answer:

Sugden Ltd
Prime cost section of the manufacturing account for the year ended 31 January 20–9

	$	$
Cost of material consumed		
Opening Inventory of raw material	58 500	
Purchases of raw material	240 800	
	299 300	
Less Closing inventory of raw materials	63 400	235 900
Direct wages		21 000
Direct expenses – Royalties		3 500
Prime cost		260 400

Types of inventory for a manufacturer

Manufacturing businesses will usually have three different types of inventory:

- raw materials – appear in the prime cost section
- work in progress (partially completed goods) – appear at the end of the manufacturing account
- finished goods – appear on the income statement in place of opening and closing inventory.

All three types of closing inventory need to be shown separately in the statement of financial position in the current assets section.

Sample question

3 The following information was provided by the Truly Scrumptious Manufacturing Company on 31 January 20–9:

	$
Carriage inwards	4 300
Carriage outwards	2 100
Factory wages	58 000
Light and heat	4 000
Inventory at 1 February 20–8:	
Raw materials	35 000
Work in progress	22 000
Finished goods	63 500
Machinery at cost	250 000
Provision for depreciation of machinery	90 000
Office equipment at cost	120 000
Provision for depreciation of office equipment	24 000
Office salaries	92 000
Insurance	6 800
Purchases of raw materials	190 000
Purchases of finished goods	15 000
Rent and rates	9 500
Royalties	1 200
Revenue	668 000

Additional information:

Inventory at 31 January 20–9:

	$
Raw materials	38 000
Work in progress	24 000
Finished goods	65 800

  i   60% of the factory wages are direct and the rest are indirect.

  ii 75% of both the light and heat and rent and rates are to be allocated to the factory and the rest to the office.

 iii 80% of the insurance cost is to be allocated to the factory.

 iv Depreciation is to be charged on the machinery at 20% using the reducing balance method.

  v   Depreciation is to be charged on the office equipment using 10% straight line method.

a Prepare a manufacturing account for the year ended 31 January 20–9.

b Prepare an income statement for the year ended 31 January 20–9.

c Prepare an extract from the statement of financial position for the inventory at 31 January 20–9.

Answer:
a

Truly Scrumptious Manufacturing Company
Manufacturing account for the year ended 31 January 20–9

	$	$
Cost of raw material consumed		
Opening inventory of raw material	35 000	
Purchases of raw material	190 000	
Carriage inwards	4 300	
	229 300	
Less Closing inventory of raw material	38 000	191 300
Direct wages		34 800
Direct expenses – Royalties		1 200
Prime cost		227 300
Factory overheads		
Indirect wages	23 200	
Depreciation of machinery	32 000	
Light and heat	3 000	
Rent and rates	7 125	
Insurance	5 440	70 765
		298 065
Add Opening work in progress		22 000
		320 065
Less Closing work in progress		24 000
Cost of production		296 065

b

Truly Scrumptious Manufacturing Company
Income statement for the year ended 31 January 20–9

	$	$
Revenue		668 000
Less Cost of sales		
Opening inventory of finished goods	63 500	
Cost of production	296 065	
Purchases of finished goods	15 000	
	374 565	
Less Closing inventory of finished goods	65 800	308 765
Gross profit		359 235
Less light and heat	1 000	
Rent and rates	2 375	
Insurance	1 360	
Depreciation of office equipment	12 000	
Office salaries	92 000	108 735
Profit for the year		250 500

Note that sometimes manufacturing companies will buy additional finished goods, perhaps to meet unexpected demand or due to a fault with machinery. These finished goods need adding to the cost of production in the cost of sales section.

c

Truly Scrumptious Manufacturing Company
Extract from statement of financial position at 31 January 20–9

	$	$
Current assets		
Inventories – Raw materials	38 000	
Work in progress	24 000	
Finished goods	65 800	127 800

Progress check

1. Name the accounting term used for partially finished goods.
2. What are the key components of the prime cost section?
3. Where does the cost of production appear on the income statement?

Examination-style questions

1. Faris manufactures all the goods he sells and provides the following information for the year:

	$
Carriage inwards	2 450
Carriage outwards	1 630
Opening inventory of raw materials	5 240
Closing inventory of raw materials	6 310
Opening inventory of work in progress	7 460
Closing inventory of work in progress	9 650
Purchases of raw materials	131 500

   What was the cost of raw materials consumed? [1]

   A $129 540
   B $130 690
   C $132 880
   D $134 510

2. The following balances were extracted from the books of Versatile Manufacturing Company on 30 September 20–9:

	$
Purchases of raw materials	135 000
Purchases of finished goods	65 500
Carriage inwards	2 300
Factory wages	64 700
Office wages	78 200
Royalties	1 725
Rent	80 000
Factory management salaries	35 600
Office management salaries	48 750
Factory indirect expenses	6 480
Factory insurance	15 000
Office expenses	4 630
Factory equipment at cost	150 000
Factory tools at cost	10 000
Provision for depreciation of factory equipment	30 000
Inventory at 1 October 20–8:	
Raw materials	15 600
Work in progress	8 800
Finished goods	36 900

   Additional information:

   i Inventory at 30 September 20–9:

	$
Raw materials	16 200
Work in progress	9 000
Finished goods	34 500

   ii Rent is allocated at 60% for factory and 40% for office.

   iii Factory insurance of £3 500 has been prepaid for the following financial year.

   iv Factory wages of $2 300 were owing.

   v The value of the factory tools at 30 September 20–9 is $8 800.

   vi Factory equipment is depreciated at the rate of 20% per annum using the reducing balance method.

   Prepare the manufacturing account for the year ended 30 September 20–9. [16]

3. The following balances were extracted from the books of Ranshaw Manufacturing on 30 November 20–8:

On 1 December 20–7	$
Factory machinery at cost	350 000
Office furniture at cost	40 000
Provision for depreciation of factory machinery	178 500
Provision for depreciation of office furniture	12 000
Inventory of raw materials	48 300
Inventory of work in progress	62 400
Inventory of finished goods	59 100
Provision for doubtful debts	1 600

For the year ended 30 November 20–8	$
Revenue	724 000
Purchases of raw materials	205 300
Purchases of finished goods	18 600
Wages and salaries	
Factory machinists	64 000
Factory supervisors	45 000
Office staff	32 500
Royalties	1 450
Rent	12 000
Insurance	3 300
Administration expenses	11 500
Commission received	6 400

At 30 November 20–8	$
Inventory of raw materials	51 000
Inventory of work in progress	64 000
Inventory of finished goods	61 100
Trade receivables	14 800
Trade payables	6 450
Bank overdraft	1 300
Owner's equity	53 800
Drawings	15 800

Additional information:

i Factory machinery is to be depreciated at 30% per annum using the reducing balance method.

ii Office furniture is to be depreciated at 15% per annum on cost.

iii A provision for doubtful debts is to be maintained at the rate of 6%.

iv Expenses are to be apportioned to the factory and office as follows:

	Factory	Office
Rent	70%	30%
Insurance	60%	40%

v Wages and salaries for the office staff of $3 200 were owing.

vi Administration expenses of $1 500 were prepaid.

  a Prepare the manufacturing account of Ranshaw Manufacturing for the year ended 30 November 20–8. Show clearly the prime cost and cost of production. [12]

  b Prepare the income statement for the year ended 30 November 20–8. [13]

  c Prepare the statement of financial position at 30 November 20–8. [11]

4 Which of the following expenses does not appear in a manufacturing account? [1]

  A carriage inwards   C office salaries

  B factory rent   D royalties

Revision checklist

In this chapter you have learnt:

- ☐ direct costs include direct materials, direct labour and direct expenses and are used to calculate prime cost: indirect costs are all other costs involved in the manufacturing of the product, also known as factory overheads

- ☐ opening work in progress is added and closing work in progress is subtracted in order to calculate the cost of production

- ☐ a manufacturing business requires a manufacturing account, income statement and a statement of financial position

- ☐ adjustments are needed for the financial statements such as allocating between the manufacturing account and income statement and calculating depreciation, provision for doubtful debts and adjusting for accrued and prepaid expenses.

Chapter 21

Limited companies

Learning summary

By the end of this chapter you should understand:

- the advantages and disadvantages of operating as a limited company
- the meaning of the term limited liability
- the meaning of the term equity
- the capital structure of a limited company comprising preference share capital, ordinary share capital, general reserve and retained earnings
- how to distinguish between issued, called-up and paid-up share capital
- how to distinguish between share capital (preference shares and ordinary shares) and loan capital (debentures)
- how to prepare income statements, statements of changes in equity and statements of financial position
- how to make adjustments to financial statements.

TERMS

Called up capital is that part of the issued share capital for which payment has been requested from shareholders.

A **debenture** is a long-term loan which has a fixed rate of interest, payable irrespective of the profit of the company.

Equity is the total funds provided by the shareholders of the company.

Issued share capital is the amount of capital issued to the shareholders.

A **limited company** is a legal entity which has a separate identity from its shareholders, whose liability for the company's debts is limited.

Paid up capital is that part of the called up share capital for which the company has received payment from shareholders.

Nature of a limited company

Sole traders or partnerships may decide to convert their businesses into limited companies. There are two types of limited company; private limited company, which can sell shares to friends and family, and public limited company, which can sell shares to the public. Shares represent that the shareholder owns a part of the limited company (equity) and their reward for owning the shares is to receive a payment called a dividend. Limited companies do not have to pay out dividends to their shareholders and may well choose to reinvest the retained earnings.

Advantages of operating as a limited company	Disadvantages of operating as a limited company
Separate legal identity from its owner	Legal requirements
Limited liability – only lose initial investment	Annual financial statements must be prepared and audited (checked by an external auditor)
Can issue shares to raise capital	Risk take-over if majority of shares sold
May find it easier to obtain loan / issue debentures	
Continuity – business continues if the original owner dies or leaves the business	

Share capital

It is important to understand the distinction between issued, called up and paid up capital. Issued capital represents the amount of shares which have been sold (issued) to shareholders. Sometimes shareholders pay for their shares in instalments and so called up capital is the amount the company has requested to be paid and paid up capital is the amount that has actually been paid for by the shareholders.

Preference shares	Ordinary shares	Debentures
Shown as a non-current liability on the statement of financial position	Owners of the business	Debenture holders make a non-current loan of capital to the business and are payables
	Receive dividends	
	Dividend is not guaranteed and is variable	
Receive a fixed rate of dividend (based on the face value)	Dividend is an appropriation of profit	Receive interest and it is fixed
Paid before ordinary shareholders	In liquidation, paid after debenture holders and preference shareholders	Interest on the loan must be paid regardless of profit for the year
In liquidation, paid before ordinary shareholders	Have voting rights	Interest is recorded on the income statement as an expense
	Can attend Annual General Meeting	In liquidation, paid before ordinary shareholders
		Do not have voting rights
		Cannot attend Annual General Meeting

TIPS

Debenture holders are not a type of shareholder. The shareholders have made a permanent investment in the business whereas a debenture loan is for a fixed time period.

Only dividends that have actually been paid appear in the statement of changes in equity, not the proposed dividends.

Differences between financial statements for sole traders, partnerships and limited companies

The key differences are as follows:

- Income statement – prepared in the same way but there may be debenture interest and dividends on redeemable preference shares.
- Statement of financial position – replace the owner's equity section or partners' capital section with an equity and reserves section which is calculated on the statement of changes in equity.
- Statement of changes in equity – this is a new financial statement specific to a limited company which shows the changes in the equity and reserves section.

Statement of changes in equity

The statement of changes in equity links figures shown on the income statement and on the statement of financial position. Profit from the year is taken from the income statement and added to the retained earnings column. Only dividends that have actually been paid, either part way through the year (interim) or at the end of the year (final), are recorded on the statement of changes in equity. It is important to remember that reserves are not necessarily cash. They represent the assets and show how they have been funded. Reasons to transfer amounts into the general reserve include:

- funds are retained for major expenditure such as purchasing non-current assets or expansion of the business
- to be used for future dividends when profits are low
- for use in emergencies or contingencies if the company has financial difficulties.

The closing balances on the statement of changes in equity then appear in the equity and reserves section of the statement of financial position.

Sample questions

1 The retained earnings for LAC Limited were $52 000 on 1 August 20–8. These had increased to $85 000 on 31 July 20–9. The company earned a profit for the year of $40 000. No dividends were to be paid.

   How much had been transferred to the general reserve for the year? [1]

   A $7 000   B $33 000   C $45 000   D $73 000

Answer:

Recreate the retained earnings column in order to solve this:

	Retained earnings $
At start	52 000
Profit for the year	40 000
Transfer to general reserve	(7 000)
At end	85 000

The answer is A, $7 000.

2 SFM Industries Limited provided the following information:

	$
At 31 January 20–7:	
Ordinary shares of $2 each	300 000
General reserve	25 000
Retained earnings	50 250
During the year ended 31 January 20–8:	
Profit for the year	26 850
Transfer to general reserve	7 500
Interim dividend paid	4 000
New shares issued	15 000
Long-term bank loan received	20 000
At 31 January 20–8:	
Non-current assets	413 750
Inventory	12 600
Trade receivables	8 900
Cash and cash equivalents	4 600
Trade payables	6 750

a Prepare the statement of changes in equity for the year ended 31 January 20–8.

b Prepare the statement of financial position at 31 January 20–8.

Answer:

a

SFM Industries Limited
Statement of changes in equity for the year ended 31 January 20–8

	Ordinary share capital $	General reserve $	Retained earnings $	Total $
Balance at 1 Feb 20–7	300 000	25 000	50 250	375 250
Share issue	15 000			15 000
Profit for the year			26 850	26 850
Dividend paid			(4 000)	(4 000)
Transfer to general reserve		7 500	(7 500)	
Balance at 31 Jan 20–8	315 000	32 500	65 600	413 100

Note how the final balances above are the same figures which appear below in the equity and reserves section.

b

SFM Industries Limited
Statement of financial position at 31 January 20–8

	$
Non-current assets (at book value)	413 750
Current assets	
Inventory	12 600
Trade receivables	8 900
Cash and cash equivalents	4 600
Total assets	26 100
	439 850
Equity and reserves	
Ordinary share capital	315 000
General reserve	32 500
Retained earnings	65 600
	413 100
Non-current liabilities	
Bank loan	20 000
Current liabilities	
Trade payables	6 750
Total liabilities	439 850

Progress check

1. State two reasons why a partnership may wish to convert into a limited company.
2. What does a debenture holder receive in return for their investment?
3. How does the statement of changes in equity link the income statement to the statement of financial position?

Examination-style questions

1. Which statement about ordinary shares is correct? [1]

   A They carry a fixed rate of dividend.

   B They carry a fixed rate of interest.

   C They carry a variable rate of dividend.

   D They carry a variable rate of interest.

2. Harvest Moon Limited provided the following information at 1 January 20–8:

	$
Ordinary share capital	300 000
General reserve	10 000
Retained earnings	89 645

   And, for the year ended 31 December 20–8:

	$
Revenue	425 000
Purchases	230 500
Heat and light	2 130
Office salaries	32 600
Rent	8 940
Other operating expenses	3 165
Dividend paid	12 000
Interest paid	6 500
Transfer to general reserve	4 000

   Inventory values were as follows:

	$
1 January 20–8	32 600
31 December 20–8	34 000

   a Prepare the income statement for the year ended 31 December 20–8. [11]

   b Prepare the statement of changes in equity for the year ended 31 December 20–8. [8]

3. Daunt Limited provided the following information:

	$
At 1 April 20–8:	
Ordinary share capital $1	80 000
General reserve	6 500
Debentures (repayable in ten years' time)	20 000
Retained earnings	32 000
For the year ended 31 March 20–9:	
Profit for the year	22 800
Interim dividend paid	3 000

   Additional information:

   i On 1 December 20–8 an additional 40 000 ordinary shares of $1 each were issued.

   ii On 31 March 20–9 the directors:
   - transferred $10 000 to the general reserve
   - paid a final ordinary dividend of $0.05 per share on all shares issued.

   a Prepare the statement of changes in equity for the year ended 31 March 20–9. [8]

   b Prepare an extract from the statement of financial position showing the equity, reserves and non-current liabilities of Daunt Limited at 31 March 20–9. [5]

4 Which type of organisation would prepare a statement of changes in equity? [1]

   A clubs and societies   C partnership
   B limited company   D sole trader

5 The trading section of the income statement for Blue Boar Limited for the year ended 30 April 20–8 showed a gross profit of $228 900.

   The following information was provided:

	$
5% bank loan repayable in four years	20 000
Cash and cash equivalents	7 520
Loan interest	500
Non-current assets	152 000
Provision for depreciation of non-current assets	77 520
Operating expenses	65 300
Retained earnings	52 850
General reserve	15 000
Ordinary share capital of $0.20 each	100 000

   Additional information which had not been entered into the books of account:

   - It is the company policy to depreciate non-current assets using the reducing balance method at the rate of 30% per annum.
   - On 12 February 20–8 the directors paid a dividend of $0.03 per share.
   - On 15 April the directors increased the general reserve by $5 000.

   a Prepare the income statement for the year ended 30 April 20–8. [4]
   b Prepare the statement of changes in equity for the year ended 30 April 20–8. [7]

Revision checklist

In this chapter you have learnt:

- ■ the advantages and disadvantages of operating as a limited company
- ■ limited liability means the shareholders lose their initial investment and not personal property, unlike sole traders and partnerships
- ■ equity replaces owner's equity on the statement of financial position
- ■ the capital structure of a limited company comprises of preference share capital, ordinary share capital, general reserve and retained earnings
- ■ to distinguish between issued, called-up and paid-up share capital
- ■ to distinguish between share capital (preference shares and ordinary shares) and loan capital (debentures)
- ■ how to prepare income statements, statements of changes in equity and statements of financial position
- ■ how to make adjustments to financial statements in the same way as for sole traders and partnerships.

Chapter 22

Analysis and interpretation

Learning summary

By the end of this chapter you should understand:

- and be able to calculate the following ratios: gross margin, profit margin, return on capital employed, current ratio, liquid (acid test) ratio, rate of inventory turnover, trade receivables turnover and trade payables turnover
- how to prepare and comment on simple statements showing comparisons of results for different years
- how to make recommendations and suggestions for improving profitability and working capital
- the significance of the difference between the gross margin and profit margin as an indicator of a business's efficiency
- the relationship of gross profit and profit for the year to the valuation of inventory, rate of inventory turnover, revenue, expenses and equity
- the problems of inter-firm comparison
- how to apply accounting ratios to inter-firm comparison
- the uses of accounting information by interested parties for decision-making
- the limitations of accounting statements.

TERMS

Liquidity ratios measure the ability of a business to turn assets into cash to pay the short term debts.

Profitability ratios measure the performance of the business by comparing the profit to other figures in the same set of financial statements.

Purpose of ratios

In addition to comparing actual figures between years and companies it is also useful for a business to carry out ratio analysis. Analysis consists of a detailed examination of the information in a set of financial statements. Interpretation is then the process of comparing the results. Accounting ratios are divided into two main groups: profitability ratios and liquidity ratios. The use of these ratios can allow a business to make a more informed decision about strategies needed to improve financial performance.

Working capital is also known as net current assets as it is the difference between current assets and current liabilities. Capital employed is the total funds which are being used by the business. It is the owner's equity plus any non-current liabilities that represents how the business has been funded.

Profitability ratios

All profitability ratios are expressed as a percentage and the business will want as high a percentage as possible for each of these ratios.

$$\text{Return on capital employed} = \frac{\text{Profit for the year before interest}}{\text{Capital employed}} \times \frac{100}{1}$$

This ratio is important as it shows the profit earned for every $100 used in the business in order to earn that profit. The higher the return, the more efficiently the capital is being employed within the business.

$$\text{Gross margin} = \frac{\text{Gross profit}}{\text{Revenue}} \times \frac{100}{1}$$

This ratio shows the gross profit earned for every $100 of sales. The higher the return, the more profitable the business.

Ways to improve gross margin	What might cause a fall in gross margin
Increase selling prices – will customers go elsewhere?	Increasing the rate of trade discount
	Selling goods at cheaper prices
Obtaining cheaper suppliers – will quality suffer?	Not passing on increased costs to customers
Increase advertising and sales promotions – will increase expenses so profit margin could fall	

$$\text{Profit margin} = \frac{\text{Profit for the year}}{\text{Revenue}} \times \frac{100}{1}$$

This ratio shows the profit earned for every $100 of sales. The higher the return, the more profitable the business.

Ways to improve profit margin	What might cause a fall in profit margin
Increasing the gross margin – see earlier section	A decrease in the gross profit
	An increase in expenses
Reduce expenses – rent cheaper property	A decrease in other income
Find cheaper lenders of finance to reduce interest charges	
Review depreciation rate	

Liquidity ratios

A business needs to be aware of its profitability but often a more pressing area to consider is that of cash. Remember profit shows what should have happened whereas cash is the reality, and it is lack of cash which often leads to the liquidation of a business rather than poor profitability. Liquidity ratios consider how easy it is to turn assets into cash.

Current ratio is shown as Current assets: Current Liabilities

Current assets are divided by current liabilities and the answer is then : 1. If current liabilities are higher than current assets it is still the same procedure but the current asset amount will be less than 1, i.e. 0.85: 1 indicates the business only has $0.85 available for each $1 owed. It compares the assets which are in the form of cash, or can be turned into cash quite easily, with the liabilities which are due within 12 months. If everyone the business owed money to in the short term demanded payment, how easy would it be to cover this with the current assets?

Problems of insufficient working capital	Ways to improve working capital
Cannot meet immediate liabilities when they are due	Introduce capital into the business
	Obtain long term loans
Hard to obtain further supplies on credit	Sell unwanted non-current assets
Cannot take advantage of cash discounts	Reduce drawings or dividends
Cannot take advantage of business opportunities when they arise	

Liquid (acid test) ratio is shown as Current assets less inventory: Current liabilities

This is the same as the current ratio but excludes inventory as this is potentially the most difficult current asset to convert into cash.

This is seen as a more accurate representation of the position of the business as some inventory may never be sold due to changes in fashion or new technology.

Rate of inventory turnover $= \dfrac{\text{Cost of sales}}{\text{Average inventory}}$

Average inventory is opening inventory plus closing inventory divided by 2. This ratio is measured as number of times. It calculates the number of times a business sells and replaces its inventory in a given period. It is essential to consider the type of product involved as a comparison cannot be made between a luxury sports car manufacturer who will have a relatively low inventory turnover and a car manufacturer who supplies basic, family models with a higher inventory turnover. Comparisons can be made between years and between similar companies.

Possible causes of a lower rate of inventory turnover:

- higher closing inventory levels – could be due to lower sales
- too high selling prices
- falling demand
- a slowdown in business activity.

Trade receivables turnover $= \dfrac{\text{Trade receivables}}{\text{Credit sales}} \times \dfrac{365}{1}$

This ratio is expressed in number of days and it is important to always round up to the nearest whole day. It measures the average time it takes credit customers to pay their accounts. A business will want this ratio to be as low as possible as this then means that credit customers are paying quicker. The longer a debt is owed, the more likely it is to become irrecoverable.

Ways to improve trade receivables turnover:

- Improve credit control policies by sending regular statements of account and stop supplying persistent late payers on credit.
- Offer cash discounts for early settlement.
- Charge interest on overdue accounts – this helps to improve profit but could encourage credit customers to look for alternative suppliers.

Trade payables turnover $= \dfrac{\text{Trade payables}}{\text{Credit purchases}} \times \dfrac{365}{1}$

This ratio is also expressed in number of days and it measures the average time taken to pay the accounts of credit suppliers. It needs to be examined alongside the trade receivables turnover as ideally a business will want the trade payables turnover days to be lower than the trade payables turnover days. Whilst a business wishes its own credit customers to pay on time, in terms of paying out to credit suppliers they may wish to delay this as long as possible so that the cash is maintained in the business. It is a difficult balancing act as the key is to delay payment without upsetting credit suppliers who could delay deliveries or incurring unnecessary interest charges.

Inter-firm comparison

It is important for a business to compare its ratios with previous years in order to make important decisions such as changes to selling prices or changes of suppliers. It is also useful to make comparisons with a similar business. It is not just about the type of product sold; it is also important that the businesses operate on a similar scale too.

Problems of inter-firm comparison include:

- differing accounting policies, for example, different methods and rates of depreciation
- some businesses may own property whilst others rent
- non-monetary items, such as skill and experience of workforce, do not appear on the financial statements but contribute to performance
- financial year-ends may be different which could have an impact on inventory levels depending on seasonality of the business
- financial statements are based on historic cost and do not show the impact of inflation.

Users of accounting information

User of accounting information	Reason for their interest
Owner(s)	Interested in both profitability and liquidity in order to assess performance and progress. This is so that vital decisions can be made which will impact on future performance. This includes shareholders if a limited company.
Managers	This may be the same person as the owner in a small business. They have the same interests as the owners as they have to make decisions and take corrective action as necessary.
Trade payables	Credit suppliers will want to know about the liquidity of the business in order to decide whether to allow trade credit, the maximum amount allowed on credit and the time period for payment.
Banks	If a business needs additional finance, such as an overdraft or a loan, then the bank manager will ask to see the financial statements in order to make their decision. They will look at the risk factor involved and will then set the interest rate and time period involved accordingly to ensure that the money has the highest chance of being repaid. Sometimes a loan will be secured (attached) to a non-current asset which can then be sold if the business cannot repay the loan.
Investors	A business may look to investors to borrow money rather than a bank, but these investors will also want to know about profitability and liquidity ratios in order to decide if their investment will be safe and will yield them a reward.
Club members	The members of a club or society will want to check that their subscriptions are being used to provide the best possible facilities. They will want any profit-making sections to at least break even and for liquidity to be secure.
Government departments	They will want to check that profit and loss reporting is correct and will also compile statistics concerning business performance and growth.
Other lenders	It is not just banks who lend money so anyone else that makes a loan to the business will want reassuring they will be repaid.
Customers	Customers will want to know that supply is guaranteed as they in turn may be supplying others and will want to be reliable.
Employees and trade unions	In order to request pay rises or improved conditions the employees and trade unions can assess the financial statements in order to judge if their demands are likely to be met. Job security can be assessed as well.

It is worth noting that the owners and managers are categorised as internal users and all other groups are external users.

Limitations of accounting statements

Ratios should not be used in isolation but rather as part of the overall judgement of how a business is performing. They do have limitations:

- Historic cost – financial transactions take place using the actual cost price and so several years later they may no longer be a fair reflection, especially if there has been a high inflation rate with costs persistently rising.
- Difficulties of definition – some businesses may use a different version of profit in their profitability ratios such as operating profit (profit before finance interest is deducted) or profit for the year. It is important to compare the same figures in order to gain the most from the ratio analysis.
- Non-financial aspects – experience and skill of staff, client lists, innovativeness and willingness to adapt to change are all hard to measure in terms of monetary terms. However, the success and future success of a business very much depend on these areas. It is the entrepreneurship of the manager and owner which drives a business forward with the appropriate funding and this is hard to put a figure on.

> **TIPS**
>
> Always ensure that ratios are expressed in the format required such as number of days or times.
>
> Learning how ratios can improve or deteriorate is just as important as learning the formulae.
>
> Ratios are one part of the analysis and interpretation of a business and must be used in conjunction with the actual financial statements of the business, knowledge about the future for the market which the business is part of and their likely contribution to further developments.

Progress check

1. State two internal and two external users of accounting information.
2. State two key differences between profitability ratios and liquidity ratios.
3. Why is return on capital employed such an important ratio to a potential investor?

Examination-style questions

1. Muthasa's accounting year ends on 30 July. The following information is available:

	20–7 $	20–8 $
Revenue	130 000	190 000
Cost of sales	98 500	112 400
Opening inventory	12 750	14 500
Expenses	19 000	20 000
Owner's equity	45 000	45 000
Long-term bank loan	35 000	30 000

Additional information:

Inventory on 30 July 20–8 was valued at $13 800.

   a Calculate the following ratios at both 30 July 20–7 and at 30 July 20–8: [8]
      i Gross profit margin
      ii Profit margin
      iii Rate of inventory turnover
      iv Return on capital employed
   b Suggest two possible reasons for the change in the profit margin over the two years. [2]

2. Malaika's accounting year ends on 30 September. The following information is available:

	$
At 30 September 20–8:	
Inventory	22 600
For the year ended 30 September 20–9:	
Revenue (all sales on credit)	420 000
Credit purchases	280 000
At 30 September 20–9:	
Inventory	25 000
Trade receivables	32 400
Bank overdraft	1 850
Trade payables	26 300

   a Calculate the current ratio. [2]
   b Calculate the liquid (acid test) ratio. [2]
   c Calculate the trade receivables turnover. [2]
   d Calculate the trade payables turnover. [2]
   e State two ways Malaika could decrease her current ratio. [2]

3. Which of the following would increase the current ratio? [1]
   A increase drawings
   B increase expenses
   C introduce more capital in cash
   D repay a long term loan

4.

	30 November 20–8	30 November 20–9
Current ratio	3.25:1	2.4:1
Liquid ratio	0.36:1	0.97:1
Trade receivables	72 days	58 days
Trade payables	28 days	35 days

Comment on the liquidity position of the company on 30 November 20–9 compared to 30 November 20–8. [6]

5. Jonah is a trader and has provided the following information on 31 May 20–7:

	$
Revenue	350 000
Purchases	180 000
Opening inventory	25 000
Closing inventory	15 000

   a State the formula and calculate the gross margin. [2]
   b State the formula and calculate the rate of inventory turnover in times. [2]
   c State two ways Jonah could improve his inventory turnover. [2]

Revision checklist

In this chapter you have learnt:

- ☐ the formulae for gross margin, profit margin, return on capital employed, current ratio, liquid (acid test) ratio, rate of inventory turnover, trade receivables turnover and trade payables turnover
- ☐ the importance of comparing ratios between years and between similar companies
- ☐ how to make recommendations and suggestions for improving profitability and working capital
- ☐ profit margin is more important overall than gross margin as it takes account of expenses too as an indicator of a business's efficiency
- ☐ the uses of accounting information by interested parties for decision-making, both internal and external
- ☐ the limitations of accounting statements due to historic cost, difficulties of definition and non-financial aspects.

Answers to examination-style questions

Introduction to accounting

1   D   [1]

2   One from: property, motor vehicle, inventory, bank, cash or trade receivables.   [1]

3

	Effect on assets	$	Effect on liabilities	$	
a	Equipment	Increase		No effect	[1]
	Cash	Decrease			[1]
b	Bank	Increase	Loan	Increase	[1]
c	Property	Increase	Mortgage	Increase	[1]
d	Inventory	Decrease			[1]
	Cash	Increase			[1]

[6]

4

Meera Traders
Statement of financial position at 1 June 20–9

	$	
Assets		
Property	160 000	[1]
Equipment	12 500	[1]
Inventory	3 440	[1]
Trade receivables	2 675	[1]
Bank	4 325	[1]
Cash	360	[1]
	183 300	[1]
Capital		
Owner's equity	128 380	[1]
Liabilities		
Bank loan	48 000	[1]
Trade payables	6 920	[1]
	183 300	[1]

[11]

5   a   Assets = $176 025   [1]

    b   Liabilities = $10 630   [1]

    c   Owner's equity = Assets – Liabilities, so, 176 025 – 10 630 = $165 395   [1]

Chapter 2

Double entry book-keeping – Part A

1.

Account debited	Account credited
Imran [1]	Sales [1]

2. To gain each mark the amount, description of account and date must be correct. [24]

Chen
Capital account

Date	Details	$	Date	Details	$
			20–8		
			Apr 1	Bank	20 000 [1]

Bank account

Date	Details	$	Date	Details	$
20–8					
Apr 1	Capital	20 000 [1]	Apr 2	Delivery van	3 500 [1]
			4	Rent	1 500 [1]
			7	Balance c/d	15 000 [1]
		20 000			20 000
8	Balance b/d	15 000 [1]			

Delivery van account

Date	Details	$	Date	Details	$
20–8					
Apr 2	Bank	3 500 [1]			

Purchases account

Date	Details	$	Date	Details	$
20–8					
Apr 3	Leak and Sons	4 400 [1]			

Leak and Sons account

Date	Details	$	Date	Details	$
20–8			20–8		
Apr 4	Purchases returns	200 [1]	Apr 3	Purchases	4 400 [1]
7	Balance c/d	4 200 [1]			
		4 400			4 400
			8	Balance b/d	4 200 [1]

Purchases returns account

Date	Details	$	Date	Details	$
			20–8		
			Apr 4	Leak and Sons	200 [1]

Rent account

Date	Details	$	Date	Details	$
20–8					
Apr 4	Bank	1 500 [1]			

Sales account

Date	Details	$	Date	Details	$
20–8			20–8		
Apr 7	Balance c/d	2 400 [1]	Apr 5	Cash	350 [1]
			7	Paul's Plumbers	2 050 [1]
		2 400			2 400
			8	Balance b/d	2 400 [1]

Cash account

Date	Details	$	Date	Details	$
20–8			20–8		
Apr 5	Sales	350 [1]	Apr 6	Wages	120 [1]
			7	Balance c/d	230 [1]
		350			350
8	Balance b/d	230 [1]			

Wages account

Date	Details	$	Date	Details	$
20–8					
Apr 6	Cash	120 [1]			

Paul's Plumbers account

Date	Details	$	Date	Details	$
20–8					
Apr 7	Sales	2 050 [1]			

3 To gain each mark the amount, description of account and date must be correct.
[31 in total]

Medi
Capital account

Date	Details	$	Date	Details	$
			20–9		
			Sept 1	Balance b/d	13 000 [1]

Motor vehicle account

Date	Details	$	Date	Details	$
20–9					
Sept 1	Balance b/d	4 200 [1]			

Machinery account

Date	Details	$	Date	Details	$
20–9			20–9		
Sept 1	Balance b/d	12 500 [1]	Sept 30	Balance c/d	16 550 [1]
30	Moriarty Ltd	4 050 [1]			
		16 550			16 550
Oct 1	Balance b/d	16 550 [1]			

Trade receivable – Lola account

Date	Details	$	Date	Details	$
20–9			20–9		
Sept 1	Balance b/d	1 890 [1]	Sept 21	Sales returns	200 [1]
			22	Bank	1 690 [1]
		1 890			1 890

Trade payable – Noah account

Date	Details	$	Date	Details	$
20–9			20–9		
Sept 4	Purchases returns	125 [1]	Sept 1	Balance b/d	1 650 [1]
30	Balance c/d	3 725 [1]	3	Purchases	2 200 [1]
		3 850			3 850
			Oct 1	Balance b/d	3 725 [1]

Loan – Lend It Finance account

Date	Details	$	Date	Details	$
20–9			20–9		
Sept 15	Bank	1 000 [1]	Sept 1	Balance b/d	4 200 [1]
30	Balance c/d	3 200 [1]			
		4 200			4 200
			Oct 1	Balance b/d	3 200 [1]

Bank account

Date	Details	$	Date	Details	$
20–9			20–9		
Sept 1	Balance b/d	260 [1]	Sept 15	Lend it Finance	1 000 [1]
8	Sales	5 600 [1]	23	Drawings	100 [1]
22	Lola	1 690 [1]	30	Balance c/d	6 450 [1]
		7 550			7 550
Oct 1	Balance b/d	6 450 [1]			

Purchases account

Date	Details	$	Date	Details	$
20–9					
Sept 3	Noah	2 200 [1]			

Purchases returns account

Date	Details	$	Date	Details	$
			20–9		
			Sept 4	Noah	125 [1]

Sales account

Date	Details	$	Date	Details	$
			20–9		
			Sept 8	Bank	5 600 [1]

Sales returns account

Date	Details	$	Date	Details	$
20–9					
Sept 21	Lola	200 [1]			

Drawings account

Date	Details	$	Date	Details	$
20–9					
Sept 23	Bank	100 [1]			

Moriarty Ltd account

Date	Details	$	Date	Details	$
			20–9		
			Sept 30	Machinery	4 050 [1]

4

Transaction	Debit		Credit	
Rent paid with cash	Rent		Cash	
Goods for resale purchased from Lomax on credit	Purchases	[1]	Lomax	[1]
Cash sales	Cash	[1]	Sales	[1]
Wages paid by cheque	Wages	[1]	Bank	[1]
Purchase of machinery by cheque	Machinery	[1]	Bank	[1]
Goods for resale purchased from Logan, with cash	Purchases	[1]	Cash	[1]
Vehicle service paid by cheque	Vehicle service	[1]	Bank	[1]
Drawings of cash	Drawings	[1]	Cash	[1]
Purchase of vehicle on credit from Daunt	Vehicle	[1]	Daunt	[1]

[16]

5   D   [1]

The trial balance

1 Trial balance for Sandeep at 31 July 20–8

	Debit $	Credit $
Rent received		10 500 [1]
Carriage inwards	525	
Carriage outwards	375 [1]	
Revenue		235 720
Purchases	111 340 [1]	
Returns inwards	3 245	
Returns outwards		6 211 [1]
Wages and salaries	32 895	
Insurance	3 190 [1]	
Cash and cash equivalents	2 200	
Fixtures and fittings	22 490 [1]	
Sundry expenses		4 498 [1]
Inventory at 1 August 2018	4 390	
Drawings	22 500 [1]	
Owner's equity		25 000 [1]
Property at cost	78 779 [1]	
	281 929	281 929

[10]

2   Trial balance for Keung at 30 April 20–8

	Debit $	Credit $
Bank overdraft		2 300
Bank loan		4 500 [1]
Owner's equity		52 000
Revenue		369 000 [1]
Purchases	152 500	
Returns inwards	2 220 [1]	
Returns outwards		480 [1]
Property at cost	180 000	
Motor vehicles at cost	99 000 [1]	
Wages and salaries		33 000 [1]
Trade receivables	4 855 [1]	
Trade payables		3 354 [1]
Rent and rates	5 600	
Drawings	12 000 [1]	
Inventory at 1 May 2017	8 459 [1]	
	464 634 [1]	464 634 [1]

[12]

3   a   Error of principle [1]

    b   Error of omission [1]

    c   Error of commission [1]

    d   Eompensating error [1]

4   An entry for a ledger account has been missed off the trial balance. [1] A ledger account has been incorrectly balanced off. [1]

5

Error	Type of error	
a	omission	[1]
b	commission	[1]
c	principle	[1]
d	complete reversal	[1]

[4]

6   B   [1]

Chapter 4

Double entry book-keeping – Part B

1 B [1]

2
Account	Ledger	
Machinery	*Nominal*	
Becca, a credit customer	Sales	[1]
Purchases	Nominal	[1]
Carriage outwards	Nominal	[1]
Luke, a credit supplier	Purchases	[1]
Drawings	Nominal	[1]

[5]

3 a

Ted's account

Date	Details	$	Date	Details	$
20–9			20–9		
Mar 1	Balance b/d	2 200 [1]	Mar 12	Sales returns	80
8	Sales	960 [1]	24	Bank	2 090 [1]
			31	Discount allowed	110 [1]
				Balance c/d	880
		3 160			3 160
Apr 1	Balance b/d	880 [1]			

[5]

b Sales ledger [1]

4 a to d

Noah
Sales ledger
Simon account

Date	Details	$	Date	Details	$
20–9			20–9		
Sept 1	Balance b/d	520 [1]	Sept 16	Bank	500 [1]
24	Bank	500 [1]	16	Discount allowed	20 [1]
			28	Bank	500 [1]
		1 020			1 020

195

Purchases ledger
Rachel account

Date	Details	$	Date	Details	$
20–9			20–9		
Sept 8	Bank	912 [1]	Sept 1	Balance b/d	960 [1]
	Discount received	48 [1]			
		960			960

Cash book

Date	Details	Discount allowed $	Cash $	Bank $	Date	Details	Discount received $	Cash $	Bank $
20–9					20–9				
Sept 1	Balances b/d		230 [1]	8 120 [1]	Sept 4	Fixtures & fittings			326 [1]
13	Sales		2 380 [1]		8	Rachel	48		912 [1]
16	Simon	20		500 [1]	14	Drawings		50 [1]	
28	Simon			500 [1]	20	Electricity			78 [1]
30	Cash c			2010 [1]	23	Rent			890 [1]
					24	Simon			500 [1]
					25	Wages		400 [1]	
					30	Bank c		2010 [1]	
					30	Balance c/d		150 [1]	8 424 [1]
		20 [1]	2610	11 130			48 [1]	2610	11 130
Oct 1	Balance b/d		150 [1]	8 424 [1]					

Nominal ledger
Fixtures and fittings account

Date	Details	$	Date	Details	$
20–9					
Sept 4	Bank	326 [1]			

Sales account

Date	Details	$	Date	Details	$
			20–9		
			Sept 13	Cash	2 380 [1]

Drawings account

Date	Details	$	Date	Details	$
20–9					
Sept 14	Cash	50 [1]			

Electricity account

Date	Details	$	Date	Details	$
20–9					
Sept 20	Bank	78 [1]			

Rent account

Date	Details	$	Date	Details	$
20–9					
Sept 23	Bank	890 [1]			

Wages account

Date	Details	$	Date	Details	$
20–9					
Sept 25	Cash	400 [1]			

Discount allowed account

Date	Details	$	Date	Details	$
20–9					
Sept 30	Total for month	20 [1]			

Discount received account

Date	Details	$	Date	Details	$
			20–9		
			Sept 30	Total for month	48 [1]

[36]

5 **Cash book (extract)**

Date	Details	Discount $	Bank $	Date	Details	Discount $	Bank $
20–9				20–9			
Mar 6	Salema	20	380 [1]	Mar 1	Balance b/d		2 200 [1]
				3	Wages		425
22	Lorna		150	15	Harrison	36	1 164 [1]
31	Loan		6 000 [1]	25	Electricity		135 [1]
				30	Lorna		150 [1]
				31	Balance c/d		2 456
		20 [1]	6 530			36	6 530
Apr 1	Balance b/d		2 456 [1]				

Chapter 5 Petty cash books

Atiqua

Petty cash book

Date	Details	Total Received $	Date	Details	Vo. no.	Total paid $	Travel $	Stationery $	Cleaning $
20–8			20–8						
Apr 1	Bal b/d	150 [1]	Apr 2	Envelopes	43	5		5 [1]	
			5	Bus fares	44	8	8 [1]		
			10	Window cleaner	45	7			7 [1]
			12	Photocopying	46	12		12 [1]	
			18	Rail ticket	47	23	23 [1]		
			21	Printer cartridge	48	34		34 [1]	
			23	Petrol	49	16	16 [1]		
			25	Bus fares	50	2	2 [1]		
			29	Cleaning cloths	51	7			7 [1]
			30	Petrol	52	22	22 [1]		
						136 [1]	71	51	14
			30	Bal c/d		14 [1]			
		150				150			
20–8									
May 1	Bal b/d	14 [1]							
	Cash	136 [1]							

[15]

Petty cash book

Date	Details	Total Received $	Date	Details	Vo. no.	Total paid $	Travel $	Postage $	Stationery $	Meals $
20–8			20–8							
Aug 1	Bal b/d	125 [1]	Aug 3	Taxi fare	33	5	5 [1]			
			6	Parcel postage	34	2		2 [1]		
			7	Pencils	35	1			1 [1]	
			9	Train fare	36	5	5 [1]			
			12	Lunch	37	12				12 [1]
			14	Large envelopes	38	2			2 [1]	
			16	Petrol	39	10	10 [1]			
			19	Meal allowance	40	5				5 [1]
			20	Recorded delivery	41	2		2 [1]		
			23	Tape	42	1			1 [1]	
			25	Excess postage	43	3		3 [1]		
			28	Taxi fare	44	6	6 [1]			
						54	26	7	4	17
			31	Bal c/d		71				
		125				125				
20–8										
Sept 1	Bal b/d	71 [1]								
	Cash	54 [1]								

Nominal ledger
Travel account

Date	Details	$	Date	Details	$
20–8					
Aug 31	Petty cash	26 [1]			

Postage account

Date	Details	$	Date	Details	$
20–8					
Aug 31	Petty cash	7 [1]			

Stationery account

Date	Details	$	Date	Details	$
20–8					
Aug 31	Petty cash	4 [1]			

Meals account

Date	Details	$	Date	Details	$
20–8					
Aug 31	Petty cash	17 [1]			

[21]

3
Marina
Petty cash book

Date	Details	Total Received $	Date	Details	Vo. no.	Total paid $	Travel $	Motor $	Stationery $	Sundry $
20–7			20–7							
Feb 1	Bal b/d	200 [1]	Feb 2	Pencils	30	4			4 [1]	
27	Refund on printer cartridge	6 [1]	5	Bus fares	31	8	8 [1]			
			10	Flowers	32	5				5 [1]
			12	Paper	33	12			12 [1]	
			18	Rail ticket	34	35	35 [1]			
			21	Printer cartridge	35	42			42 [1]	
			23	Petrol	36	16		16 [1]		
			25	Bus fares	37	4	4 [1]			
			26	Cleaning materials	38	7				7 [1]
			28	Petrol	39	19		19 [1]		
						152	47	35	58	12
			28	Bal c/d		54 [1]				
		206 [1]				206 [1]				
20–7										
Mar 1	Bal b/d	54 [1]								
	Cash	146 [1]								

[20]

4 C [1]

5 At the end of the period, the total of each expense analysis column [1] is transferred to the appropriate ledger account [1] and the individual entries in the ledger account column [1] are transferred to the personal accounts of the credit suppliers [1].

Business documents

1. a. i. Sales invoice [1]

   ii. Credit note [1]

   b. Statement of account [1]

2.

Transaction	Source document	Account to debit	Account to credit
Bought goods on credit from Solo Ltd	*Purchase invoice*	*Purchases*	*Solo Ltd*
Sold goods on credit to Rayner	Sales invoice [1]	Rayner [1]	Sales [1]
Rayner returned some faulty goods	Credit note [1]	Sales returns [1]	Rayner [1]
Bought goods for cash	Receipt [1]	Purchases [1]	Cash [1]

[9]

3.

Seasons greetings   Invoice 468
Unit 4a
New Business Park   Tel: 01856 342698
Shoreham-by-Sea
SH14 6UT

12 April 20–9

Invoice to:
News Are Us
The Precinct
Shoreham-by-Sea
SH23 8AH

Product	Quantity	Unit price $	Amount $
Greeting cards various	150	0.60	90 [1]
Wrapping paper metallic	44	2.25	99 [1]
Gift tags – pack of 10	60	1.10	66 [1]
Glitter spray	80	3.10	248 [1]
			503 [1]
Terms: 5% cash discount if account paid by 30 April 20–9		Less 15% trade discount	75.45 [1]
		Amount payable	427.55 [1]

$406.17 will be paid if cash discount is received [1]

[8]

4 C [1]

5

	Document	
A demand for payment	Invoice	[1]
A written acknowledgement of money received	Receipt	[1]
A summary of transactions for a period issued to a customer	Statement of account	[1]
Issued by a purchaser of goods on credit to request a reduction in the invoice received	Debit note	[1]

[4]

Books of prime entry

Chapter 7

1

Source document	Book of prime entry	
Cheque counterfoil	*Cash book*	
Sales invoice	Sales journal	[1]
Credit note received	Purchases returns journal	[1]
Purchase invoice	Purchases journal	[1]
Credit note issued	Sales returns journal	[1]

[4]

2

Transaction	Book of prime entry		Account to be debited		Account to be credited	
Bought goods on credit from Maurizio	*Purchases journal*		*Purchases*		*Maurizio*	
Paolo returned goods	Sales returns journal	[1]	Paolo	[1]	Sales returns	[1]
Paid rent by standing order	Cash book	[1]	Rent	[1]	Bank	[1]
Sold goods to Roman for cash	Cash book	[1]	Cash	[1]	Sales	[1]
Sold goods to Becca on credit	Sales journal	[1]	Becca	[1]	Sales	[1]

[12]

3

Purchase ledger
Sid account

Date	Details	$		Date	Details	$	
20–8				20–8			
Apr 6	Purchases returns	120	[1]	Apr 1	Balance b/d	560	
29	Discount received	28	[1]	3	Purchases	672	[1]
29	Bank	532	[1]	18	Purchases	320	[1]
30	Balance c/d	872					
		1 552				1 552	
				May 1	Balance b/d	872	[1]

[6]

203

4 a

Quaid
Purchases journal

Date	Name	Invoice number	Amount $
20–9			
Oct 1	Kate	1956	1 760 [1]
13	Sienna	1112	1 300 [1]
31	Transfer to purchases account		3 060

Purchases returns journal

Date	Name	Credit note number	Amount $
20–9			
Oct 8	Kate	C 1032	32 [1]
16	Sienna	C 50	75 [1]
31	Transfer to purchases returns account		107

Sales journal

Date	Name	Invoice number	Amount $
20–9			
Oct 1	Emily	1432	3 910 [1]
16	Emily	1433	2 890 [1]
31	Transfer to sales account		6 800

Sales returns journal

Date	Name	Credit note number	Amount $
20–9			
Oct 15	Emily	C 59	1 020 [1]
31	Transfer to sales returns account		1 020

b

Purchases ledger
Kate account

Date	Details	$	Date	Details	$
20–9			20–9		
Oct 8	Purchases returns	32 [1]	Oct 1	Purchases	1 760 [1]

Sienna account

Date	Details	$	Date	Details	$
20–9			20–9		
Oct 28	Purchases returns	75 [1]	Oct 13	Purchases	1 300 [1]

Nominal ledger
Purchases account

Date	Details	$	Date	Details	$
20–9					
Oct 31	Credit purchases for month	3 060 [1]			

Purchases returns account

Date	Details	$	Date	Details	$
			20–9		
			Oct 31	Returns for month	107 [1]

Sales ledger
Emily account

Date	Details	$	Date	Details	$
20–9			20–9		
Oct 4	Sales	3 910 [1]	Oct 15	Sales returns	1 020 [1]
16	Sales	2 890 [1]			

Nominal ledger
Sales account

Date	Details	$	Date	Details	$
			20–9		
			Oct 31	Credit sales for month	6 800 [1]

Sales returns account

Date	Details	$	Date	Details	$
20–9					
Oct 31	Returns for month	1 020 [1]			

[18]

5 A [1]

Chapter 8: Financial statements – Part A

1 B [1]

2
	Trading business only	Service business only	Both
Opening inventory	✓ [1]		
Gross profit	✓ [1]		
Loan interest			✓ [1]
Loss for the year			✓ [1]

[4]

3
Blooming Wildly Garden Centre
Income statement (trading section) for the year ended 31 March 20–9

	$	$	$
Revenue		512 830 [1]	
Less Sales returns		6 953 [1]	505 877 [1]
Less Cost of sales			
Opening inventory		25 630 [1]	
Purchases	342 400 [1]		
Less Purchases returns	2 560 [1]		
	339 840		
Carriage inwards	3 400 [1]	343 240	
Less Closing inventory		21 568 [1]	347 302 [1]
Gross profit			158 575 [1]

[10]

4

George
Income statement for the year ended 31 December 20–8

	$	$
Revenue	76 945 [1]	
Less Sales returns	2 900 [1]	74 045 [1]
Less Cost of sales		
Opening inventory	5 870 [1]	
Purchases	43 982 [1]	
Carriage inwards	852 [1]	
Less Purchases returns	1 400 [1]	
Less Closing inventory	6 485 [1]	42 819 [1]
Gross profit		31 226 [1]
Less Expenses		
Property tax	1 600 [1]	
Wages	13 055 [1]	14 655 [1]
Profit from operations		16 571 [1]
Less Loan interest		950 [1]
Profit for the year		15 621 [1]

[15]

5

Sales account

Date	Details	$	Date	Details	$
20–8			20–8		
Dec 31	Income statement	23 440 [1]	Dec 1	Bal b/d	16 593
			31	Total to date	6 847 [1]
		23 440			23 440

Sales returns account

Date	Details	$	Date	Details	$
20–8			20–8		
Dec 1	Bal b/d	1 279	Dec 31	Income statement	1 557 [1]
31	Total to date	278 [1]			
		1 557			1 557

Purchases account

Date	Details	$	Date	Details	$
20–8			20–8		
Dec 1	Bal b/d	10 349	Dec 31	Income statement	14 873 [1]
31	Total to date	4 524 [1]			
		14 873			14 873

Purchases returns account

Date	Details	$	Date	Details	$
20–8			20–8		
Dec 31	Income statement	1 198 [1]	Dec 1	Bal b/d	1 049
			31	Total to date	149 [1]
		1 198			1 198

Ashlin Trading
Income statement (trading section) for the month ended 31 December 20–8

	$	$
Revenue	23 440 [1]	
Less Sales returns	1 557 [1]	
		21 883 [1]
Less Cost of sales		
Opening inventory	2 650 [1]	
Purchases	14 873 [1]	
Less Purchases returns	1 198 [1]	
Carriage inwards	782 [1]	
Less Closing inventory	2 478 [1]	14 629 [1]
Gross profit		7 254 [1]

[18]

Financial statements – Part B

1 C [1]

2 Current assets [1]

3

Transaction	Assets $	Liabilities $	Capital $
Purchased a motor vehicle on credit for $5 500	+5 500	+5 500	No effect
Sold goods on credit for $900 (cost $500)	+400 [1]	No effect [1]	+400 [1]
Obtained a bank loan for $10 000	+10 000 [1]	+10 000 [1]	No effect [1]
Paid a trade payable, $300, by cheque	–300 [1]	–300 [1]	No effect [1]

[9]

4 a

Abdul
Trial balance at 31 March 20–8

	$	$
Motor vehicle	5 520 [1]	
Trade receivables	11 600 [1]	
Trade payables		6 320 [1]
Capital		18 280 [1]
Equipment	5 500 [1]	
Inventory at 1 April 20–7	2 500 [1]	
Wages and salaries	7 920 [1]	
Purchases	26 320 [1]	
Revenue		42 680 [1]
Bank	220 [1]	
Cash	160 [1]	
Rent	1 320 [1]	
Sales returns	1 640 [1]	
Purchases returns		1 120 [1]
Fixtures and fittings	2 200 [1]	
General expenses	800 [1]	
Discounts allowed	2 080 [1]	
Discounts received		1 480 [1]
Drawings	2 100 [1]	
	69 880 [1]	69 880 [1]

[21]

b   Abdul
Income statement for the year ended 31 March 20–8

	$	$
Revenue	42 680 [1]	
Less Sales returns	1 640 [1]	
		41 040 [1]
Less Cost of sales		
Opening inventory	2 500 [1]	
Purchases	26 320 [1]	
Less Purchases returns	1 120 [1]	
Less Closing inventory	3 200 [1]	24 500 [1]
Gross profit		16 540 [1]
Add Discount received		1 480 [1]
		18 020 [1]
Less Expenses		
Wages and salaries	7 920 [1]	
Rent	1 320 [1]	
General expenses	800 [1]	
Discount allowed	2 080 [1]	12 120 [1]
Profit for the year		5 900 [1]

[17]

c

Abdul
Statement of financial position at 31 March 20–8

Assets	$
Non-current assets	
Equipment	5 500 [1]
Fixtures and fittings	2 200 [1]
Motor vehicle	5 520 [1]
	13 220 [1]
Current assets	
Inventory	3 200 [1]
Trade receivables	11 600 [1]
Bank	220 [1]
Cash	160 [1]
	15 180 [1]
Total assets	28 400 [1]
Capital and liabilities	
Capital	
Opening balance	18 280 [1]
Plus Profit for the year	5 900 [1]
Less Drawings	2 100 [1]
	22 080 [1]
Current liabilities	
Trade payables	6 320 [1]
Total capital and liabilities	28 400 [1]

[16]

5 a Trial balance = $194 325 [1] so the missing capital = $85 350 [1]

b

Coral
Income statement for the year ended 31 October 20–7

	$	$
Income from lessons		98 500 [1]
Less Expenses		
Insurance	3 600 [1]	
Cleaning expenses	420 [1]	
Electricity	830 [1]	
Advertising	1 600 [1]	6 450
Profit from operations		92 050
Less loan interest		90 [1]
Profit for the year		91 960 [1]

c

Coral
Statement of financial position at 31 October 20–7

	$
Assets	
Non-current assets	
Property	180 000 [1]
Dance equipment	5 300 [1]
	185 300
Current assets	
Cash	125 [1]
Total assets	185 425
Capital and liabilities	
Capital	
Opening balance	85 350 [1]
Plus Profit for the year	91 960 [1]
Less Drawings	2 360 [1]
	174 950
Non-current liabilities	
Loan	10 000 [1]
Current liabilities	
Bank overdraft	475 [1]
Total capital and liabilities	185 425

[15]

Accounting rules

Chapter 10

1. Purchase of machinery, motor vehicle or any other non-current assets or a specific improvement to a non-current asset, such as installing air conditioning. [1]

2. The answer is A as inventory is a current asset. [1]

3.

Transaction	Revenue Expenditure	Revenue Receipt	Capital Expenditure	Capital Receipt
Sold motor vehicle				✓ [1]
Paid rent	✓ [1]			
Took out a ten–year bank loan				✓ [1]
Bought machinery to use in the business			✓ [1]	
Sold inventory		✓ [1]		
Repainted factory gates	✓ [1]			

[5]

4.

Proposed action	Principle	
Provide for trade debts which are probably irrecoverable	*Prudence*	
Value inventory at lower of cost or net realisable value	Prudence	[1]
Continue to use straight line depreciation method	Consistency	[1]
The owner records money they take out of the business as drawings	Business entity	[1]
A new air conditioning unit is being recorded as a non-current asset	Materiality	[1]

[4]

5.

	Overstated	Understated
Gross profit for the year	$155 [1]	
Profit for the year	$155 [1]	
Current assets	$155 [1]	

[3]

213

Chapter 11

Other payables and other receivables

1 a $26 700 [1]

   b Saffy owed rent of $2 000 [1]

   c
Saffy
Rent account

Date	Details	$	Date	Details	$
20–8			20–8		
Oct 3	Bank	12 000 [1]	Oct 1	Balance b/d	2 000
20–9			20–9		
Jan 2	Bank	8 500 [1]	Sep 30	Income statement	26 700 [1]
May 4	Bank	10 500 [1]	30	Balance c/d	2 300
		31 000			31 000
Oct 1	Balance b/d	2 300 [1]			

[5]

2
Sheniya
Rent receivable account

Date	Details	$	Date	Details	$
20–8			20–8		
Nov 1	Balance b/d	4 200	Dec 31	Bank	12 200 [1]
20–9			20–9		
Feb 12	Bank	500 [1]	Mar 31	Bank	9 150 [1]
Oct 31	Income statement	20 000 [1]	Oct 31	Balance c/d	3 350
		24 700			24 700
Nov 1	Balance b/d	3 350 [1]			

[5]

3 a

Nigel
Rent and rates expenses account

Date	Details	$	Date	Details	$
20–7			20–7		
Dec 1	Balance b/d rates	1 050 [1]	Dec 1	Balance b/d rent	3 800 [1]
20–8			20–8		
Nov 30	Bank rent	18 500 [1]	Nov 30	Income statement rent	13 500 [1]
	Bank rates	9 200 [1]		Income statement rates	9 400 [1]
				Balance c/d rent	1 200
				Balance c/d rates	850
		28 750			28 750
Dec 1	Balance b/d rent	1 200 [1]			
	Balance b/d rates	850 [1]			

[8]

b

Nigel
Extract from statement of financial position at 30 November 20–8

Current assets [1]	$
Other receivables	2 050 [1]

[2]

4 A [1]

5 a

Nabeegh
Income statement for the year ended 31 December 20–7

	$	$
Revenue		128 450 [1]
Less Sales returns		680 [1]
		127 770
Opening inventory	10 750 [1]	
Purchases	92 500 [1]	
	103 250	
Less Purchases returns	946 [1]	
	102 304	
Less Closing inventory	11 300 [1]	
Cost of sales		91 004 [1]
Gross profit		36 766 [1]
Rent received		6 550 [1]
Discount received		1 800 [1]
		45 116
Less Expenses		
Insurance	465 [1]	
Wages	34 380 [1]	
Discount allowed	2 200 [1]	
Office expenses	746 [1]	37 791
Profit from operations		7 325
Loan interest		320 [1]
Profit for the year		7 005 [1]

b

Nabeegh
Statement of financial position at 31 December 20–7

	$	$
Assets		
Non-current assets		
Property		195 000 [1]
Fixtures and fittings		3 690 [1]
		198 690
Current assets		
Inventory	11 300 [1]	
Trade receivables	7 200 [1]	
Other receivables	1 705 [1]	20 205
Total assets		218 895
Capital and liabilities		
Capital		
Opening balance		196 500 [1]
Plus Profit for the year		7 005 [1]
Less Drawings		4 500 [1]
		199 005
Non-current liabilities		
4% loan repayable in 6 years		8 000 [1]
Current liabilities		
Bank overdraft	2 500 [1]	
Trade payables	6 690 [1]	
Other payables	2 700 [1]	11 890
Total capital and liabilities		218 895

[28]

Chapter 12

Accounting for depreciation and disposal of non-current assets

1. The straight line method is calculated using the cost of the non-current asset [1] and has the same charge each year [1]. The reducing balance method is calculated using the net book value of the non-current asset [1] and results in a lower amount of depreciation each year [1]. The revaluation method compares the value of the non-current assets at the start of the year and at the end [1] and the difference is the depreciation charge for the year [1].

   The reducing balance method [1] would be most appropriate for the machinery as the decrease in depreciation charge each year would be matched for the increase in maintenance and replacing parts, etc. [1]

   [8]

2. a

   Now Ltd
   Fixtures and fittings account

Date	Details	$	Date	Details	$
20–7			20–7		
1 Jan	Balance b/d	42 000 [1]	1 Apr	Bank	3 100 [1]
1 Apr	Bank	15 200 [1]	31 Dec	Balance c/d	54 100 [1]
		57 200			57 200
20–8					
1 Jan	Balance b/d	54 100 [1]			

   [5]

   b 54 100 [1] × 0.2 = $10 820 [1]

3. a

Year 1	15 000 × 0.3	4 500 [1]
Year 2	10 500 × 0.3	3 150 [1]
Total		7 650 [1]

   [3]

   b

   Shavaiz
   Motor vehicle account

Date	Details	$	Date	Details	$
20–9			20–9		
1 Jan	Balance b/d	15 000 [1]	27 June	Disposal	15 000 [1]
27 June	Bank	19 500 [1]	31 Dec	Balance c/d	19 500
		34 500			34 500
20–0					
1 Jan	Balance b/d	19 500 [1]			

Provision for depreciation of motor vehicle account

Date	Details	$	Date	Details	$
20–9			20–9		
27 June	Disposal	7 650 [1]	1 Jan	Balance b/d	7 650 [1]
31 Dec	Balance c/d	5 850	31 Dec	Income statement	5 850 [1]
		13 500			13 500
			20–0		
			1 Jan	Balance b/d	5 850 [1]

Motor vehicle disposal account

Date	Details	$	Date	Details	$
20–9			20–9		
27 June	Motor vehicle	15 000 [1]	27 June	Provision for depreciation	7 650 [1]
31 Dec	Income statement [1]	900 [1]		Cash	8 250 [1]
		15 900			15 900

Plus 1 mark for dates and years.

[14]

4 A [1]

5 a

Uday
Income statement for the year ended 31 May 20–7

	$	$
Revenue		185 000 [1]
Opening inventory	10 350 [1]	
Purchases	76 500 [1]	
	86 850	
Carriage inwards	1 040 [1]	
	87 890	
Less Closing inventory	9 700 [1]	
Cost of sales		78 190 [1]
Gross profit		106 810 [1]
Commission receivable		3 275 [1]
Discount received		1 800 [1]
		111 885
Less Expenses		
Depreciation for fixtures and fittings	405 [1]	
Depreciation for delivery van	1 536 [1]	
General expenses	2 320 [1]	
Motor expenses	1 920	
Wages	43 240 [1]	
Discounts allowed	635	
Lighting and heating	1 080	
Loss on disposal of fixtures and fittings	115 [1]	51 251
Profit for the year		60 634 [1]

b

Uday
Statement of financial position at 31 May 20–7

	$ Cost	$ Accumulated depreciation	$ Net book value
Assets			
Non-current assets			
Property	180 000	–	180 000 [1]
Fixtures and fittings	4 050	2 070	1 980 [1]
Delivery van	15 000	8 856	6 144 [1]
			188 124
Current assets			
Inventory		9 700 [1]	
Trade receivables		3 480 [1]	
Other receivables		280 [1]	
Cash and cash equivalents		4 460 [1]	17 920
			206 044
Total assets			
Capital and liabilities			
Capital			
Opening balance			147 000 [1]
Plus Profit for the year			60 634 [1]
Less Drawings			4 500 [1]
			203 134
Current liabilities			
Trade payables			1 860 [1]
Other payables			1 050 [1]
Total capital and liabilities			206 044

Chapter 13: Irrecoverable debts and provisions for doubtful debts

1 D [1]

2
Rose
Provision for doubtful debts account

Date	Details	$	Date	Details	$
20–9			20–8		
May 31	Balance c/d	2 750 [1]	June 1	Balance b/d	2 300 [1]
			20–9		
			May 31	Income statement	450 [1]
		2 750			2 750
			June 1	Balance b/d	2 750 [1]

[4]

3
Kian Ltd
Sales ledger – Fox Ltd

Date	Details	$	Date	Details	$
20–8			20–8		
Jan 1	Balance b/d	4 800 [1]	Dec 31	Irrecoverable debts	4 800 [1]
		4 800			4 800

Nominal ledger
Irrecoverable debts account

Date	Details	$	Date	Details	$
20–8			20–8		
Dec 31	Fox Ltd	4 800 [1]	Dec 31	Income statement	4 800 [1]
		4 800			4 800

Debts recovered account

Date	Details	$	Date	Details	$
20–8			20–8		
Dec 31	Income statement	2 500 [1]	Dec 31	Bank (HLP Ltd)	2 500 [1]
		2 500			2 500

Provision for doubtful debts account

Date	Details	$	Date	Details	$
20–8			20–8		
Dec 31	Balance c/d	17 500 [1]	Jan 1	Balance b/d	11 500 [1]
			Dec 31	Income statement	6 000 [1]
		17 500			17 500
			20–9		
			Jan 1	Balance b/d	17 500 [1]

Kian Ltd
Extract from income statement for the year ended 31 December 20–8

	$
Gross profit	XXX
Add Debt recovered	2 500 [1]
Expenses – Irrecoverable debts	4 800 [1]
Increase in provision for doubtful debts	6 000 [1]

Extract from statement of financial position at 31 December 20–8

	$	$
Current assets		
Trade receivables	350 000 [1]	
Less Provision for doubtful debts	17 500 [1]	332 500 [1]

[16]

4 a
Destiny Diva
Income statement for the year ended 31 August 20–8

	$	$
Fees from clients		14 500 [1]
Reduction in provision for doubtful debts		45 [1]
		14 545
Less Expenses		
Insurance	1 050 [1]	
Make-up expenses	4 970 [1]	
Irrecoverable debts	120 [1]	
Motor vehicle expenses	1 580 [1]	
Loan interest	200 [1]	
Depreciation of motor vehicle	1 920 [1]	
Depreciation of office equipment	500 [1]	
		10 340
Profit for the year		4 205 [1]

[10]

b

Destiny Diva
Statement of financial position at 31 August 20–8

	$	$
Assets		
Non-current assets		
Motor vehicles at cost	12 000	
Less Provision for depreciation	4 320	7 680 [1]
Office equipment at cost	5 000	
Less Provision for depreciation	1 500	3 500 [1]
		11 180
Current assets		
Trade receivables	4 500	
Less Provision for doubtful debts	135	4 365 [1]
Other receivables		250 [1]
Bank		5 810 [1]
Cash		120 [1]
		10 545
Total assets		21 725
Capital and liabilities		
Capital		
Opening balance		25 000 [1]
Plus Profit for the year		4 205 [1]
Less Drawings		13 000 [1]
		16 205
Non-current liabilities		
Loan		5 000 [1]
Current liabilities		
Other payables		520 [1]
Total capital and liabilities		21 725

[11]

5

Riley
Sales ledger
Arthur

Date	Details	$	Date	Details	$
20–8			20–8		
May 1	Balance b/d	1 200 [1]	July 6	Bank	1 200 [1]
Aug 20	Sales	450 [1]	20–9		
			Mar 24	Irrecoverable debt	450 [1]
		1 650			1 650

224

Nominal ledger
Irrecoverable debts account

Date	Details	$	Date	Details	$
20–9			20–9		
Mar 24	Arthur	450 [1]	May 31	Income statement	450 [1]
		450			450

Debts recovered account

Date	Details	$	Date	Details	$
20–9			20–8		
May 31	Income statement	200 [1]	Sep 1	Bank (Denise)	200 [1]
		200			200

Provision for doubtful debts account

Date	Details	$	Date	Details	$
20–9			20–8		
May 31	Income statement	250 [1]	June 1	Balance b/d	1 450 [1]
	Balance c/d	1 200 [1]			
		1 450			1 450
			20–9		
			June 1	Balance b/d	1 200 [1]

[12]

Chapter 14

Bank reconciliation statements

1 B [1]

2 a

Cash book (bank columns)

Date	Details	$	Date	Details	$
20–9			20–9		
Aug 1	Balance b/d	722	Aug 1	Bank charges	25 [1]
				R Oliver dishonoured	236 [1]
				Sansa Gas	165 [1]
				Balance c/d	296 [1]
		722			722
Aug 1	Balance b/d	296 [1]			

[5]

b

Farah
Bank reconciliation statement at 31 July 20–9

	$	$
Balance at bank as shown in cash book		296 [1]
Add Cheques not yet presented:		
L Turner	805 [1]	
Carters	623 [1]	
Free Ways	65 [1]	1 493
		1 789
Less Amounts not yet credited:		
Strangeways		354 [1]
Balance at bank as shown on bank statement		1 435 [1]

[6]

3 a

Cash book (bank columns)

Date	Details	$	Date	Details	$
20–9			20–9		
June 1	Best Value Co	680 [1]	June 1	Balance b/d	890 [1]
				Insurance	320 [1]
				Phones For All	90 [1]
	Balance c/d	666 [1]		Bank charges	46 [1]
		1 346			1 346
			June 1	Balance b/d	666 [1]

[7]

b

Dragon Fire Ltd
Bank reconciliation statement at 31 May 20–9

	$
Balance at bank as shown in cash book	(666) [1]
Add Cheques not yet presented	625 [1]
Less Amounts not yet credited	1 070 [1]
Balance at bank as shown on bank statement	(1 111) [1]

[4]

4

	Cash book or bank reconciliation?	Debit or credit (for cash book entries)	
Bank interest received	Cash book	Debit	[1]
Cash sales not yet credited	Bank reconciliation [1]		
Direct debit for telephone	Cash book	Credit	[1]
Standing order for rent	Cash book	Credit	[1]
Unpresented cheque	Bank reconciliation [1]		
Dishonoured cheque	Cash book	Credit	[1]

[6]

5 a

Cash Book (bank columns)

Date	Details	$	Date	Details	$
20–9			20–9		
April 1	Bank interest	20 [1]	April 1	Balance b/d	890 [1]
	Imran	320 [1]		Water	170 [1]
	Electricity	165 [1]		Rent	780 [1]
	Balance c/d	1 335			
		1 840			1 840
			April 1	Balance b/d	1 335 [1]

[7]

b

Charlene
Bank Reconciliation Statement at April 1 20–9

	$
Balance at bank as shown in cash book	(1 335) [1]
Add Cheques not yet presented:	
Damon	805 [1]
Less Amounts not yet credited:	
Cash sales	975 [1]
Balance at bank as shown on bank statement	(1 505) [1]

[4]

Journal entries and correction of errors

Chapter 15

1 There have been two errors here. First of all the entry should be a debit in an expense account and secondly the amount is incorrect. We need to remove the credit entry by debiting travel expenses with $350 and then enter the correct amount, $280 debit, so that is $630 in total to debit the travel expenses account. The question does not state that the error occurred elsewhere so the credit entry is suspense $630, answer D.

[1]

2 a

Nehal
Trial balance at 31 March 20–8

	Debit $	Credit $
Machinery	18 700	
Trade payables		3 300
Inventory	4 620	
Revenue		31 500
Purchases	24 400	
Cash and cash equivalents	2 100	
Owner's equity		15 000
Trade receivables	2 700	
Bank loan		10 000
Suspense [1]	7 280 [1]	
	59 800 [1]	59 800 [1]

[4]

b

General journal

	Debit $	Credit $
Purchases	7 000 [1]	
Suspense		7 000 [1]
Cash and cash equivalents	280 [1]	
Suspense		280 [1]

[4]

229

3 a

Shreya
Suspense account

Details	$	Details	$
Balance b/d	140 [1]	Travel expenses	260 [1]
Discount received	400 [1]	Sales	700 [1]
Discount allowed	400 [1]		
Electricity	20 [1]		
	960		960

[6]

b
General journal

	Debit $	Credit $
Machinery	2 500	
Machinery repairs		2 500 [1]
B James	350 [1]	
B Jones		350
Bank charges	15 [1]	
Bank		15 [1]

[4]

4 a
General journal

	Debit $	Credit $
Rent payable		2 900 [1]
Rent receivable		2 900 [1]
Suspense	5 800 [1]	
Light and heat	90 [1]	
Suspense		90 [1]
Suspense	4 200 [1]	
Sales		4 200 [1]

b
Orlando
Suspense account

Details	$	Details	$
Rent payable	2 900 [1]	Balance b/d	9 910 [1]
Rent receivable	2 900 [1]	Light and heat	90 [1]
Sales	4 200 [1]		
	10 000		10 000

[12]

230

5 Dipika
Statement of correction of gross profit for the year ended 30 July 20–8

	No effect	Increase $	Decrease $	$
Draft gross profit				32 500
Error i			320 [1]	
Error ii			250 [1]	
Error iii		300 [1]		
Error iv	✓ [1]			
		300	570	
Corrected gross profit				32 230 [1]

[5]

Chapter 16: Control accounts

1 B [1]

2

Fred
Nominal ledger
Sales ledger control account

Date	Details	$	Date	Details	$
20–8			20–9		
June 1	Balance b/d	8 200 [1]	May 31	Sales returns	2 100 [1]
20–9				Bank	100 305 [1]
May 31	Sales	102 050 [1]		Discount allowed	1 600 [1]
				Irrecoverable debts	585 [1]
				Contra	250 [1]
				Balance c/d	5 410
		110 250			110 250
June 1	Balance b/d	5 410 [1]			

Fred
Nominal ledger
Purchases ledger control account

Date	Details	$	Date	Details	$
20–9			20–8		
May 31	Purchases returns	1 845 [1]	June 1	Balance b/d	6 500 [1]
	Bank	76 480 [1]	20–9		
	Discount received	980 [1]	May 31	Purchases	84 520 [1]
	Contra	250 [1]		Balance c/d	500
	Balance c/d	11 965			
		91 520			91 520
June 1	Balance b/d	500 [1]	June 1	Balance b/d	11 965 [1]

[16]

3

Amandeep
Nominal ledger
Sales ledger control account

Date	Details	$	Date	Details	$
20–9			20–9		
Jan 1	Balance b/d	580 [1]	Dec 31	Sales returns	280 [1]
	Sales	9 365 [1]		Bank	8 700 [1]
				Irrecoverable debt	145 [1]
				Balance c/d	820
		9 945			9 945
20–0					
Jan 1	Balance b/d	820 [1]			

[6]

4

Keung
Nominal ledger
Purchases ledger control account

Date	Details	$	Date	Details	$
20–8			20–8		
Mar 31	Purchases returns	915 [1]	Mar 1	Balance b/d	42 500 [1]
	Bank	64 950 [1]	31	Purchases	84 360 [1]
	Discount received	1 410 [1]		Balance c/d	130
	Contra	850 [1]			
	Balance c/d	58 865			
		126 990			126 990
			20–8		
Apr 1	Balance b/d	130 [1]	Apr 1	Balance b/d	58 865 [1]

[8]

5 Entry in sales ledger control account

	Debit	Credit	Source of information	
Returns by credit customers		✓	Sales returns journal	[1]
Discount allowed		✓	Cash book	[1]
Receipts from credit customers		✓	Cash book	[1]
Interest charged to customer on overdue account	✓		Journal	[1]
Dishonoured cheque	✓		Cash book	[1]
Irrecoverable debts written off		✓	Journal	[1]
Refunds to credit customers	✓		Cash book	[1]

[7]

Incomplete records

1

Ricado
Total trade payables account

Date	Details	$	Date	Details	$
20–9			20–8		
Aug 31	Purchases returns	185 [1]	Sept 1	Balance b/d	890 [1]
	Bank	5 640 [1]	20–9		
	Discount received	300 [1]	Aug 31	Purchases	6 230 [1]
	Balance c/d	995			
		7 120			7 120
			Sept 1	Balance b/d	995 [1]

[6]

2

Max
Income statement (trading section) for the year ended 31 January 20–9

	$	$
Revenue		900 000 [1]
Less Cost of sales		
Opening inventory	40 000 [1]	
Purchases	685 000 [1]	
	725 000	
Less Closing inventory	50 000 [1]	675 000 [1]
Gross profit		225 000 [1]

[6]

3   Kiyoko
   Statement of financial position at 28 February 20–9

Assets	Cost $	Acc dep $	Net book value $
Non-current assets	8 200	4 205 [1]	3 995 [1]
Current assets			
Inventory			820 [1]
Trade receivables			620 [1]
			1 440
Total assets			5 435
Capital and liabilities			
Capital			
Opening balance			6 200 [1]
Plus Profit for the year			895 [1]
Less Drawings			3 050 [1]
			4 045
Current liabilities			
Trade payables			745 [1]
Other payables			230 [1]
Bank overdraft			415 [1]
			1 390
Total capital and liabilities			5 435

[10]

4 A   [1]

5 a

Vicky Hoang
Income statement for the year ended 30 June 20–7

	$	$
Revenue		444 375 [1]
Opening inventory	6 000 [1]	
Purchases	361 500 [1]	
	367 500	
Less Closing inventory	12 000	
Cost of sales		355 500 [1]
Gross profit		88 875 [1]
Less Expenses		
Business expenses	51 870 [1]	
Depreciation for delivery van	2 000 [1]	53 870
Profit for the year		35 005 [1]

[8]

b

Vicky Hoang
Statement of financial position at 30 June 20–7

	$ Cost	$ Accumulated depreciation	$ Net book value
Assets			
Non-current assets			
Delivery van	12 000	2 000	10 000 [1]
Current assets			
Inventory		12 000 [1]	
Other receivables		450 [1]	
Cash and cash equivalents		12 075 [1]	24 525
Total assets			34 525
Capital and liabilities			
Capital			
Opening balance			13 520 [1]
Plus Profit for the year			35 005 [1]
Less Drawings			20 500 [1]
			28 025
Current liabilities			
Trade payables			6 500 [1]
Total capital and liabilities			34 525

[8]

Accounts of clubs and societies

1 B [1]

2

Staley Chess Club
Subscriptions account

Date	Details	$	Date	Details	$
20–8			20–8		
Nov 1	Balance b/d	320 [1]	Nov 1	Balance b/d	480 [1]
20–9			20–9		
Oct 31	Income and expenditure	9 475 [1]	Oct 31	Bank	9 200 [1]
				Irrecoverable debts	320 [1]
	Balance c/d	390 [1]		Balance c/d	185 [1]
		10 185 [1]			10 185 [1]
Nov 1	Balance b/d	185 [1]	Nov 1	Balance b/d	390 [1]

[11]

3

Ambleside Climbing Society
Statement of financial position at 30 April 20–7

	$	$
Assets		
Non-current assets		6 500 [1]
Equipment		
Current assets	1 600 [1]	
Inventory	365 [1]	
Subscriptions owed	145 [1]	
Other receivables	695 [1]	2 805 [1]
Bank		9 305 [1]
Total assets		
Accumulated funds and liabilities		
Accumulated fund		5 870 [1]
Opening balance		420 [1]
Plus Surplus for the year		6 290 [1]
Non-current liabilities		2 000 [1]
6% bank loan repayable 20–9		
Current liabilities	235 [1]	
Trade payables	260 [1]	
Other payables	520 [1]	
Subscriptions prepaid		1 015 [1]
		9 305 [1]
Total liabilities		

[16]

4 a
Ashton Football Club
Receipts and payments account for the year ended 31 July 20–8

Receipts		$		Payments	$
20–7			20–8		
Aug 1	Balance b/d	8 200 [1]	July 31	Payments to suppliers	4 500
20–8				Purchase of new equipment	4 630 [1]
July 31	Subscriptions	12 620		Rent sportsground	3 600
	Receipts from café-bar	5 650 [1]		Wages of coach	2 820 [1]
				Other operating expenses	1 935 [1]
				Balance c/d	8 985
		26 470			26 470
Aug 1	Balance b/d	8 985 [1]			

[6]

b
Ashton Football Club
Subscriptions account

Date	Details	$	Date	Details	$
20–8			20–7		
July 31	Income & expenditure [1]	13 140 [1]	Aug 1	Balance b/d	300 [1]
			20–8		
			July 31	Bank	12 620 [1]
				Balance c/d	220
		13 140			13 140
Aug 1	Balance b/d	220 [1]			

[5]

c
Ashton Football Club
Calculation of café profit for the year ended 31 July 20–8

	$	$
Sales		5 650 [1]
Opening inventory	965	
Purchases (4 500 [1] – 420 [1] + 385 [1])	4 465	
Closing inventory	840 [1]	
Cost of sales		4 590
Profit for the year		1 060 [1]

[6]

d

Ashton Football Club
Income and expenditure account for the year ended 31 July 20–8

Income	$	$
Subscriptions		13 140 [1]
Café-bar profit		1 060 [1]
		14 200
Expenditure		
Rent paid for sports ground	3 600 [1]	
Wages of coach	2 820 [1]	
Other operating expenses	1 935 [1]	
Depreciation of equipment (4 200 + 4 630 – 6 830)	2 000 [2]	10 355
Surplus for the year		3 845 [1]

[8]

e

Ashton Football Club
Statement of financial position at 31 July 20–8

	Cost	Accumulated depreciation	Net book value
	$	$	$
Non-current assets			
Sports equipment	8 830 [1]	2 000 [1]	6 830 [1]
Current assets			
Shop inventory		840 [1]	
Subscriptions owed		220 [1]	
Bank		8 985 [1]	
		10 045	
Total assets			16 875
Accumulated funds and liabilities			
Accumulated fund			
Opening balance			12 645 [1]
Plus Surplus for the year			3 845 [1]
Current liabilities			16 490
Trade payables			385 [1]
Total liabilities			16 875

[9]

Chapter 19 Partnerships

1   B   [1]

2

Mittzy, Sue and Karl
Profit and loss appropriation account for the year ended 31 July 20–8

		$	$	
Profit for the year			64 800	[1]
Add Interest on drawings	Mittzy	200		
	Sue	125		
	Karl	165	290	[1]
			65 290	
Less Interest on capital	Mittzy	4 680		
	Sue	2 520		
	Karl	5 730	(12 930)	[1]
			52 360	
Less Partner's salary	Mittzy	10 000		
	Karl	15 000	(25 000)	[1]
			27 360	
Profit share	Mittzy	104 [1]		
	Sue	104 [1]		
	Karl	572 [1]	27 360	

                                                                                               [7]

3   a   Hiroshi's capital = $45 500   [1]

         Mitsu's capital = $15 300   [1]

b

Hiroshi and Mitsu
Statement of financial position at 1 March 20–9

	$	$
Non-current assets		
Property		25 000
Motor vehicle	9 500	
Machinery	16 800	51 300 [1]
Current assets		
Inventory	7 000	
Trade receivables	4 350	
Cash and cash equivalents	3 400 [1]	14 750 [1]
		66 050
Capital – Hiroshi	45 500 [1]	
– Mitsu	15 300 [1]	60 800
Current liabilities		
Trade payables		5 250 [1]
		66 050

[6]

4 a

Anthony and Beatrix
Appropriation account for the year ended 31 August 20–9

		$	$
Profit for the year			58 000
Less Interest on capital	Anthony	10 500 [1]	
	Beatrix	7 500 [1]	
			18 000
			40 000
Profit share	Anthony	30 000 [1]	
	Beatrix	10 000 [1]	
			40 000

b

Anthony and Beatrix
Capital accounts

Date	Details	A $	B $	Date	Details	A $	B $
20–9				20–8			
31 Aug	Bal c/d	70 000	60 000 [1]	1 Sep	Bal b/d	70 000	40 000 [1]
				20–9			
				1 Feb	Bank	70 000	20 000 [1]
		70 000	60 000			70 000	60 000
				1 Sep	Bal b/d		60 000 [1]

c

Current accounts

Date	Details	A $	B $	Date	Details	A $	B $
20–8				20–8			
1 Sep	Bal b/d	1 800 [1]		1 Sep	Bal b/d		4 300 [1]
20–9				20–9			
31 Aug	Drawings	28 500 [1]	19 800	31 Aug	Interest on capital	3 300	3 600 [1]
	Bal c/d	3 000			Profit share	30 000	10 000 [1]
					Bal c/d		1 900
		33 300	19 800			33 300	19 800
1 Sep	Bal b/d		1 900 [1]	1 Sep	Bal b/d	3 000 [1]	

[15]

5 a **Arthur and Charlotte**
Income statement for the year ended 31 December 20–9

	$	$
Revenue		680 000 [1]
Less Sales returns		2 000 [1]
		678 000
Opening inventory	28 500 [1]	
Purchases	320 000	
	348 500	
Less Purchases returns	3 200 [1]	
	345 300	
Less Closing inventory	31 000 [1]	
Cost of sales		314 300
Gross profit		363 700 [1]
Profit on disposal of fixtures		200 [1]
		363 900
Less Expenses		
Irrecoverable debt	2 800 [1]	
Increase in provision for doubtful debts	300 [1]	
Depreciation for motor vehicle	6 400 [1]	
Depreciation for fixtures and fittings	1 950 [1]	
Wages and salaries	26 800 [1]	
Electricity and water	1 500	
Insurance	2 050 [1]	
Motor vehicle expenses	1 750	
General expenses	22 500	
		66 050
Profit from operations		297 850
Loan interest		1 050 [1]
Profit for the year		296 800
Add Interest on drawings		
Arthur	400	
Charlotte	600	1 000 [1]
		297 800
Less Interest on capital		
Arthur	4 800	
Charlotte	3 600	8 400 [1]
		289 400
Less Salary for Charlotte		9 400 [1]
		280 000
Profit share		
Arthur	168 000 [1]	
Charlotte	112 000 [1]	280 000

[19]

b

Current accounts

Date	Details	A $	C $	Date	Details	A $	C $
20–9				20–9			
1 Jan	Bal b/d		980	1 Jan	Bal b/d	1 500 [1]	
31 Dec	Drawings	4 000 [1]	6 000	31 Dec	Interest on capital	4 800	3 600 [1]
	Interest on drawings	400	600 [1]		Salary		9 400 [1]
	Balance c/d	169 900	117 420		Profit share	168 000 [1]	112 000
		174 300	125 000	20–0		174 300	125 000
				1 Jan	Balance b/d	169 900 [1]	117 420 [1]

c

Arthur and Charlotte
Statement of financial position at 31 December 20–9

	$ Cost	$ Accumulated depreciation	$ Net book value
Assets			
Non-current assets			
Property	382 945		382 945
Motor vehicle	50 000	24 400	25 600 [1]
Fixtures and fittings	19 500	5 850	13 650 [1]
			422 195
Current assets			
Inventory		31 000 [1]	
Trade receivables	30 000		
Provision for doubtful debts	1 500		
Other receivables		28 500 [1]	
Cash and cash equivalents		250 [1]	
Total assets		4 800 [1]	64 550
			486 745
Capital			
Arthur		80 000 [1]	
Charlotte		60 000 [1]	140 000
Current			
Arthur		169 900 [1]	
Charlotte		117 420 [1]	287 320
Non-current liabilities			
7% bank loan repayable in five years			15 000
Current liabilities			
Trade payables		43 500	
Other payables		925 [1]	44 425
Total capital and liabilities			486 745

[19]

Manufacturing accounts

1 C [1]

2
Versatile Manufacturing Company
Manufacturing account for the year ended 30 September 20–9

	$	$
Cost of raw material consumed		
Opening inventory of raw material	15 600 [1]	
Purchases of raw material	135 000 [1]	
Carriage inwards	2 300 [1]	
	152 900	
Less Closing inventory of raw material	16 200 [1]	136 700
Direct wages		67 000 [1]
Direct expenses – Royalties		1 725 [1]
Prime cost		205 425 [1]
Factory overheads		
Management salaries	35 600 [1]	
Indirect expenses	6 480 [1]	
Insurance	11 500 [1]	
Rent	48 000 [1]	
Depreciation of equipment	24 000 [1]	
Depreciation of tools	1 200 [1]	91 180
		296 605
Add Opening work in progress		8 800 [1]
		305 405
Less Closing work in progress		9 000 [1]
Cost of production		296 405 [1]

[16]

3 a Ranshaw Manufacturing
Manufacturing account for the year ended 30 November 20–8

	$	$
Cost of raw material consumed		
Opening inventory of raw material	48 300 [1]	
Purchases of raw material	205 300 [1]	
	253 600	
Less Closing inventory of raw material	51 000 [1]	202 600
Direct wages – Factory machinists		64 000 [1]
Direct expenses – Royalties		1 450 [1]
Prime cost		268 050
Factory overheads		
Wages and salaries of supervisors	45 000 [1]	
Insurance	1 980 [1]	
Rent	8 400 [1]	
Depreciation of machinery	51 450 [1]	106 830
		374 880
Add Opening work in progress		62 400 [1]
		437 280
Less Closing work in progress		64 000 [1]
Cost of production		373 280 [1]

[12]

b

Ranshaw Manufacturing
Income statement for the year ended 30 November 20–8

	$	$
Revenue		724 000 [1]
Less Cost of sales		
Opening inventory of finished goods	59 100 [1]	
Cost of production	373 280 [1]	
Purchases of finished goods	18 600 [1]	
	450 980	
Less Closing inventory of finished goods	61 100 [1]	389 880
Gross profit		334 120
Decrease in provision for doubtful debts		712 [1]
Commission received		6 400 [1]
		341 232
Less Wages and salaries of office staff	35 700 [1]	
Rent	3 600 [1]	
Insurance	1 320 [1]	
Depreciation of office equipment	6 000 [1]	
Administration and finance	10 000 [1]	56 620
Profit for the year		284 612 [1]

[13]

c

Ranshaw Manufacturing
Statement of financial position at 30 November 20–8

	Cost $	Accumulated Depreciation $	Net book value $
Assets			
Non-current assets			
Factory machinery	350 000	229 950	120 050 [1]
Office furniture	40 000	18 000	22 000 [1]
	390 000	247 950	142 050
Current assets			
Inventory – Raw materials	51 000		
Work in progress	64 000		
Finished goods	61 100	176 100 [1]	
Trade receivables	14 800		
Provision for doubtful debts	888	13 912 [1]	
Other receivables		1 500 [1]	191 512
Total assets			333 562
Capital and liabilities			
Capital			
Opening balance			53 800 [1]
Plus Profit for the year			284 612 [1]
Less Drawings			15 800 [1]
			322 612
Current liabilities			
Trade payables		6 450 [1]	
Other payables		3 200 [1]	
Bank overdraft		1 300 [1]	10 950
Total capital and liabilities			333 562

[11]

4 C [1]

Limited companies

1 C [1]

2 a
Harvest Moon Limited
Income statement for the year ended 31 December 20–8

	$	$
Revenue		425 000 [1]
Cost of sales		
Opening inventory	32 600 [1]	
Purchases	230 500 [1]	
	263 100	
Less Closing inventory	34 000 [1]	229 100
Gross profit		195 900 [1]
Less Expenses		
Heat and light	2 130 [1]	
Office salaries	32 600 [1]	
Rent	8 940 [1]	
Other operating expenses	3 165 [1]	46 835
Operating profit		149 065
Finance costs		6 500 [1]
Profit for the year		142 565 [1]

[11]

b
Harvest Moon Limited
Statement of changes in equity for the year ended 31 December 20–8

	Ordinary share capital $	General reserve $	Retained earnings $	Total $
Balance at 1 Jan 20–8	300 000	10 000	89 645	399 645
Profit for the year			142 565 [1]	142 565
Dividend paid			(12 000) [1]	(12 000)
Transfer to general reserve		4 000 [1]	(4 000) [1]	
Balance at 31 Dec 20–8	300 000 [1]	14 000 [1]	216 210 [1]	530 210 [1]

[8]

3 a

Daunt Limited
Statement of changes in equity for the year ended 31 March 20–9

	Ordinary share capital $	General reserve $	Retained earnings $	Total $
Balance at 1 Apr 20–8	80 000	6 500	32 000	118 500
Share issue	40 000 [1]			40 000
Profit for the year			22 800 [1]	22 800
Interim dividend paid			(3 000) [1]	(3 000)
Final dividend paid			(7 000) [1]	(7 000)
Transfer to general reserve		10 000 [1]	(10 000) [1]	
Balance at 31 March 20–9	120 000 [1]	16 500	34 800	171 300 [1]

[8]

b

Daunt Limited
Extract from the statement of financial position at 31 March 20–9

	$
Equity and reserves	
Ordinary shares	120 000 [1]
General reserve	16 500 [1]
Retained earnings	34 800 [1]
	171 300 [1]
Non-current liabilities	
Debentures	20 000 [1]
	191 300

[5]

4 B [1]

5 a

Blue Boar Limited
Income statement for the year ended 30 April 20–8

	$	$
Gross profit		228 900
Less Expenses		
Depreciation of non-current assets	22 344 [1]	
Operating expenses	65 300 [1]	87 644
Operating profit		141 256
Finance costs		1 000 [1]
Profit for the year		140 256 [1]

[4]

b

Blue Boar Limited
Statement of changes in equity for the year ended 30 April 20–8

	Ordinary share capital	General reserve	Retained earnings	Total
	$	$	$	$
Balance at 1 May 20–7	100 000	15 000	52 850	167 850 [1]
Profit for the year			140 256 [1]	140 256
Dividend paid			15 000 [1]	15 000
Transfer to general reserve		5 000 [1]	(5 000) [1]	
Balance at 30 April 20–8	100 000	20 000 [1]	203 106 [1]	323 106

[7]

Chapter 22

Analysis and interpretation

1 a

		20–7 $	20–8 $
i	Gross profit margin	24.23% [1]	40.84% [1]
ii	Profit margin	9.62% [1]	30.32% [1]
iii	Rate of inventory turnover	7.23 times [1]	7.94 times [1]
iv	Return on capital employed	15.63% [1]	76.80% [1]

[8]

b Increased selling price. [1]
Cheaper cost of sales due to better discounts achieved. [1]
Any other reasonable explanation.

2 a Current ratio = current assets: current liabilities = 57 400: 28 150 [1] = 2.04: 1 [1]
b Liquid (acid test) ratio = current assets − inventory: current liabilities
32 400: 28 150 [1] = 1.15: 1 [1]

c Trade receivables turnover = $\dfrac{\text{trade receivables}}{\text{credit sales}} \times 365 = \dfrac{32\,400}{420\,000}$ [1] = 29 days [1]

d Trade payables turnover = $\dfrac{\text{trade payables}}{\text{credit purchases}} \times 365 = \dfrac{26\,300}{280\,000}$ [1] = 35 days [1]

e Two of the following: increase drawings, [1] reduce inventory held, [1] increase payables. [1]

3 C [1]

4 If inventory is not included then there are insufficient short term assets to cover current liabilities [1]. This has improved over the year and they now have $0.97 available for every $1 owed. [1] Too high a proportion of current assets is made up of inventory, though this again has improved and indicates they are keeping less inventory [1]. Holding large amounts of inventory can increase storage costs, security and wastage [1]. It also ties up cash which could be used elsewhere [1].

Trade receivables turnover has improved as it is now taking 58 days for trade receivables to pay, rather than 72 days [1]. However, this is still higher than the trade payables turnover at 35 days. To aid liquidity and cash flow, the trade receivables turnover should be lower than the trade payables turnover [1]. Increasing trade payables turnover could damage the relationship with credit suppliers [1]. Insisting on faster payments from credit customers could lead to loss of sales [1].

Maximum of 6 marks for any of the above points.

5 a $\dfrac{\text{Gross profit}}{\text{Revenue}} \times 100$ [1] = $\dfrac{160\,000}{350\,000} \times 100 = 45.71\%$ [1]

b $\dfrac{\text{Cost of sales}}{\text{Average inventory}}$ [1] = $\dfrac{190\,000}{20\,000} = 9.5$ times [1]

c Keep lower amounts of closing inventory. [1]
Reduce selling prices. [1]

Answers to progress check questions

Chapter 1

1. Book-keeping is the detailed recording of all the financial transactions of a business. Accounting uses these book-keeping records to prepare financial statements.
2. Assets – Liabilities = Owner's equity
3. Assets are items owned by the business or owed to it.

   Liabilities represent what is owed by the business.

   Owner's equity is the total resources provided by the owner and represents what the business owes the owner.
4. The assets and liabilities of a business on a certain date.

Chapter 2

1. In order to record the two aspects of every transaction, each transaction is entered twice. The account which is receiving or gaining the value is debited and the account which is giving the value is credited.
2. Inventory.
3. Reduce it.
4. The trade receivable account is debited rather than the cash account.

Chapter 3

1. A list of balances on the accounts in the ledger at a certain date.
2. It simply means that the total debit balances equal the total of the credit balances. It does not mean the double entry is error-free.
3. Error of commission – cash received from Jones and credited to Johnson's account.

   Error of complete reversal – cash sales debited to the sales account and credited to the cash account.

   Error of omission – payment of rent not entered in the books.

   Error of original entry – goods sold on credit for $400 but recorded as $4000.

   Error of principle – equipment bought to use in the business is debited to the purchases account.

   Compensating errors – drawings account is under-added by $200 and wages account is over-added by $200.
4. The uses of a trial balance is that it can help in locating arithmetical errors and to prepare financial statements. The limitation is that it is no proof that the ledger accounts are completely free from errors and there may be any one of six errors hidden within the trial balance which will still mean that it balances.

Chapter 4

1. A two column cash book contains the cash and bank accounts and the three column cash book has the same but also a cash discount column.
2. If it is an overdraft.
3. Insufficient funds in the trade receivables account or an error on the cheque, such as no date or no signature.
4. They are both payments made via the bank account but the person paying controls the amount of the standing order and the person receiving controls the direct debit.

Chapter 5

1. Low value items such as travel expenses or stationery for the office.
2. This is where the amount spent each period is restored so that the petty cashier starts each period with the same amount.
3. Cleaning, stationery and travel expenses.

Chapter 6

1. A debit note is not entered in the accounting records and is a request for a reduction in the invoice received. A credit note is entered in the accounting records and is issued by the seller of the goods to notify of a reduction in an invoice previously issued.
2. A document issued by the seller of goods on credit to summarise the transactions for the month.
3. Both represent proof of purchase or sale.

Chapter 7

1. Sales journal, purchases journal, sales returns journal and purchases returns journal.
2. To record credit sales.
3. Over ordered or faulty.
4. To the sales account and purchases account in the nominal ledger.

Chapter 8

1. A service business provides a service and only prepares the profit and loss account section of the income statement, whereas a trading business buys and sells goods and uses the trading account section as well as the profit and loss account section of the income statement.
2. A statement prepared for a trading period to show the gross profit and profit for the year.
3. The trial balance.

Chapter 9

1. A non-current liability is an amount owed by the business and not due for repayment within the next 12 months, whereas current liabilities are short-term and due for repayment within the next 12 months.
2. To show the assets and liabilities of a business on a certain date.
3. Tangible non-current assets are long-term assets which are obtained for use rather than for resale and can be touched, whereas intangible non-current assets do not have material substance, they cannot be seen or touched.

Chapter 10

1. Capital expenditure is money spent by a business on purchasing or improving non-current assets, whereas revenue expenditure is money spent on running a business day-to-day.
2. Revenue receipts = revenue from sale of goods or rent received.

    Capital receipts = receipt of capital from the owner or the receipt of loans.
3. To see if they are improving compared to previous years or performing better than competition.
4. Inventory is always valued at the lower of cost or net realisable value.

Chapter 11

1. An accrued expense is an expense relating to a particular accounting period which is unpaid at the end of that period, whereas accrued income is income which has not been received.
2. In the income statement an accrued expense is added to the total paid and a prepaid expense is deducted. The accrued expense appears as a current liability and the prepaid expense as a current asset on the statement of financial position.
3. Prepaid income is income received which relates to a future accounting period so it does not yet belong to the business.

Chapter 12

1. Disposal account.
2. Small items of equipment used in offices, crockery, loose tools where no detailed records are kept.
3. Debit the income statement and credit the provision for depreciation account.

Chapter 13

1. Prudence.
2. Added to gross profit with any other income received.

3. This ranks the trade receivables according to how long they have owed the business so that the business can prioritise who they chase for payment.
4. It is an income item if the provision has decreased and an expense item if the provision has increased.

Chapter 14

1. A dishonoured cheque appears on the credit side of the cash book in the bank column.
2. Timing issues, errors and amounts paid directly into and out of the bank, such as bank charges or direct debits.
3. Timing differences, items not known so not yet entered in the cash book as direct debits, dishonoured cheques, items paid directly into the bank account.

Chapter 15

1. Error of commission, error of complete reversal, error of omission, error of original entry, error of principle and compensating errors.
2. Suspense account.
3. Opening entries, purchases and sales of non-current assets on credit and correction of errors.

Chapter 16

1. Assist in locating errors when the trial balance fails to balance and provide a summary of the transactions affecting the trade receivables and trade payables for each financial period.
2. The amount owed by trade receivables at the end of the financial period.
3. The business may have overpaid or paid a deposit for goods not yet received so the supplier owes the business.

Chapter 17

1. Using a total trade receivables account.
2. More informed decision-making is possible and information required by banks or lenders is readily available.
3. If a cash purchase occurs then no trade payable is created as the business is paid straight away.

Chapter 18

1. Accumulated fund.
2. Clubs and societies are not formed with the primary aim of creating a profit so a surplus arises when the gains exceed the expenses.
3. Current liabilities section.

Chapter 19

1. Additional finance; knowledge, experience and skills; responsibilities and risks are shared and discussions can take place.
2. Drawings, interest on drawings and interest on capital.
3. This then minimises the amount of external finance which will need to be borrowed and interest rates on loans could be significantly higher.

Chapter 20

1. Work in progress.
2. Direct materials, direct labour and direct expenses.
3. It is in place of the purchases in the trading account section.

Chapter 21

1. Limited liability means the owners only lose the amount invested and not their personal possessions and in order to gain additional finance through the sale of shares.
2. Interest each year and then the original amount invested returned at the end of the period agreed.
3. Profit for the year comes from the income statement, which is then added to retained profit on the statement of changes in equity, which then appears on the statement of financial position.

Chapter 22

1. Two internal are owners and managers. Two external are trade payables and bank managers.
2. Liquidity ratios are concerned with cash and the ability of a business to pay what they owe and they do not necessarily indicate profitability. Profitability ratios do assess profitability but do not demonstrate the ability of a business to survive in the short term.
3. It allows potential investors to compare what their likely return will be from their investment as it shows how efficiently the capital is being employed within the business.

Index

accounting, definition 2–3
accounting equation 4–5
accounting rules 76–80
accounting statements
   limitations 182
   users 183
accrued expenses 83–4
accrued income 83, 87–8
accumulated fund 143, 148
analysis and interpretation
   inter-firm comparison 181
   liquidity ratios 178, 179–81
   profitability ratios 178, 179
analysis columns 35
appropriation accounts 154, 156
assets 2, 4, 6
   see also current assets; non-current assets

balance brought down 13
balance carried down 13
balances
   credit 15–16, 130
   debit 15, 130
   definition 9
balancing ledger accounts 12–13
bank accounts 13, 27
bank charges 109
bank interest 109
bank overdrafts 26
bank reconciliation statements 108–9
bank statements 108–9
banks 182
book-keeping 2–3
   see also double entry book-keeping
books of prime entry 50–1
business entity principle 76, 78

called up capital 171, 172
capital (owner's equity)
   definition 2, 3, 6
   in partnership agreements 155
capital accounts 157
capital employed 178
capital expenditure 76, 79–80
capital receipts 76, 79
carriage 9
carriage inwards 9, 11, 15, 22, 62
carriage outwards 9, 11, 15, 22, 62

cash
   in statements of financial position 70
   not yet credited 108
cash books
   contra entries in 26, 27, 29
   items not recorded in 109
   three column 28–9
   two column 27
   see also petty cash books
cash discount 26, 28–9, 45
cash floats 35
cash purchases 13, 137
cash sales 13, 137
cheques
   definition 44
   dishonoured 26, 29, 109
   not yet presented 108
   use of 47–8
closing inventory 62, 73, 78
clubs and societies
   accumulated fund 143, 148
   as non-trading organisations 143–4
   income and expenditure accounts 143, 145
   members 182
   membership subscriptions 143, 149
   receipts and payments accounts 143, 144
   statements of financial position 148
   trading section of income statements 145
combined expense accounts 86
comparability of financial statements 79
compensating errors 19, 22, 120
consistency principle 76, 78
contra entries
   in cash books 26, 27, 29
   in control accounts 127, 131
control accounts
   advantages 127
   balances on both sides of 130
   contra entries 127, 131
   purchases ledger 127, 129
   purpose 127
   sales ledger 127, 128
correction of errors 120–2
cost of inventory 80
cost of production 162
counterfoils 48
credit balances 15–16, 130
credit cards 27

credit notes 44, 46, 52
credit purchases 14, 137
credit sales 14, 137
credit side of a ledger account 9–10, 11
credit transfers 47, 109
current accounts 157
current assets 69, 70, 180
current liabilities 2, 69, 180
current ratio 180
customers 182

dates, in ledger accounts 11
debentures 171, 172
debit balances 15, 130
debit cards 27
debit notes 44, 46
debit side of a ledger account 9–10, 11
debts
    irrecoverable 100–1, 104, 118
    provision for doubtful 100, 101, 104, 119
    written off 100, 101
decision-making 3
deficits 143
depletion of non-current assets 92
depreciation
    causes 91–2
    definition 91
    methods of calculating 92–3
    recording in the financial statements 95, 97
    recording in the ledger 93
direct debits 27, 109
discount
    cash 26, 28–9, 45
    trade 26, 29, 45
dishonoured cheques 26, 29, 109
disposal of non-current assets 96–7
dividends 109, 171
double entry book-keeping 9–16, 26–9
    see also ledger accounts
drawers 47
drawings 9, 12, 62, 155
drawings accounts 12
duality principle 77, 78

economic reasons for depreciation 92
electronic payments 27
employees 182
equity 171
errors
    compensating 19, 22, 120
    correction of 120–2

    of commission 19, 22, 120
    of complete reversal 19, 22, 120
    of omission 19, 22, 120
    of original entry 19, 22, 120
    of principle 19, 22, 120
expense accounts 15–16, 86
expenses, accrued and prepaid 83–4

financial statements 60–5, 69–73
finished goods 164
fixed capital accounts 157
floats, cash 35

general journals see journals (general journals)
general ledgers (nominal ledgers) 26, 27
going concern principle 76, 77
goods
    finished 164
    in ledger accounts 11
    returned 14, 51, 52
goodwill 69
government departments 182
gross margin 179

historic cost principle 76, 78
historic costs 92, 183

imprest system 35–6
income, accrued and prepaid 83, 87–8
income accounts 16
income and expenditure accounts 143, 145
income statements
    definition 3, 60
    effect of correcting errors on 122
    importance of 61
    of limited companies 173
    of service businesses 61
    of trading businesses 61
    profit and loss section of 62
    recording depreciation in 95
    trading section of 61–2, 145
    transferring ledger account totals to 62–3
incomplete records 135–40
interest
    bank 109
    in partnership agreements 155
    on loans 62, 155
inter-firm comparison 181
inter-ledger transfers (contra entries) 127, 131
international accounting standards 79

inventory
   closing 62, 73, 78
   in statements of financial position 70
   manufacturing 164
   opening 62
   turnover 135, 138, 180
   valuation 80
investors 182
invoices 44–5
irrecoverable debts 100–1, 104, 118
issued share capital 171, 172

journals (general journals)
   correction of errors 120–2
   definition 116
   non-regular transactions 118–19
   opening entries 117
   purchase and sale of non-current assets 117
   purpose 116

ledger accounts
   balancing 12–13
   credit and debit sides 9–10, 11
   dates in 11
   interpreting 15–16
   of partnerships 157
   recording carriage inwards and carriage outwards in 15
   recording sales, purchases and returns in 13–14
   transferring totals to income statements 62–3
   see also cash books; nominal ledgers (general ledgers); purchases ledgers; sales ledgers
ledgers, definition 9
lenders 182
liabilities 2, 4, 6, 69, 180
lifespan of non-current assets 92
limited companies
   advantages and disadvantages 172
   definition 171
   financial statements 173
   private and public 171
   share capital 172
   trial balances for 22
liquid (acid test) ratio 180
liquidity ratios 178, 179–81
list price 52
loan interest 62, 155
loss 2, 3
loss for the year 62

managers 182
manufacturing accounts 162–4
manufacturing overheads 162
margin 135, 138
mark-up 135, 138
matching principle 76, 77–8
materiality principle 76, 78
membership subscriptions 143, 149
money measurement principle 77, 78
monitoring progress 3

net book value 91, 93
net current assets (working capital) 178, 180
net realisable value of inventory 80
nominal ledgers (general ledgers) 26, 27
non-current asset accounts 93
non-current assets
   definition 2, 69
   disposal of 96–7
   in statements of financial position 70
   lifespan 92
   recording purchase and sale of 117
   return of 14
   see also depreciation
non-current liabilities 2, 69
non-regular transactions 118–19
non-trading organisations 143–4
   see also clubs and societies

opening inventory 62
opening journal entries 117
ordinary shares 172
overdrafts, bank 26
overheads, manufacturing 162
owners, business 182
owner's equity see capital (owner's equity)

paid up capital 171, 172
partnership agreements 154, 155
partnerships
   advantages and disadvantages of 155
   appropriation accounts 154, 156
   definition 154
   ledger accounts 157
   statements of financial position 158
   trial balances for 22
payees 47
petty cash books 35–6
petty cash vouchers 35
physical deterioration of non-current assets 92
preference shares 172

prepaid expenses 83–4
prepaid income 83, 87–8
prime cost 162
prime entry, books of 50–1
principle of duality 77, 78
private limited companies 171
production, cost of 162
profit
   definition 2
   for the year 62
   from operations 62
   measuring 3
   residual 154
profit and loss section of income statements 62
profit for the year 62
profit/loss sharing ratio 155
profit margin 179
profitability ratios 178, 179, 183
progress monitoring 3
provision for depreciation accounts 93
provision for doubtful debts 100, 101, 104, 119
prudence principle 77, 78, 80
public limited companies 171
purchase invoices 45
purchases, calculating 137
purchases accounts 13–14
purchases journals 51, 54
purchases ledger control accounts 127, 129
purchases ledgers 26, 27
purchases returns 14
purchases returns journals 51, 54

rate of inventory turnover 135, 138, 180
ratio analysis 178
raw materials 164
realisation principle 77, 78
receipts 44, 48
receipts and payments accounts 143, 144
recovery of debts written off 101
reducing balance method of depreciation 91, 93
relevance of financial statements 79
reliability of financial statements 79
residual profit 154
residual value 91
return on capital employed 179
returned goods 14, 51, 52
revaluation method of depreciation 91, 93
revenue expenditure 77, 79–80
revenue receipts 77, 79

salaries, partnership 155
sales, calculating 137
sales accounts 13–14
sales invoices 44
sales journals 51, 52
sales ledger control accounts 127, 128
sales ledgers 26, 27
sales returns 14
sales returns journals 51, 52
service businesses 60, 61
set-offs (contra entries) 127, 131
share capital 171, 172
shareholders 171–2
shares 109, 171
societies see clubs and societies
sole traders 60–1
standing orders 27, 109
statements of account 44, 47
statements of affairs 135, 136
statements of changes in equity 173
statements of financial position
   content 5
   definition 3, 69
   effect of correcting errors on 122
   importance of 69
   inter-relationship of items 70
   layout 70
   of clubs and societies 148
   of limited companies 173
   of partnerships 158
straight line method of depreciation 91, 92, 93
subscriptions, membership 143, 149
sundry expenses 38, 40
surpluses 143
suspense accounts 116

three column cash books 28–9
time, depreciation over 92
timing differences, and bank statements 108
total accounts see control accounts
total trade payables accounts (purchases ledger control accounts) 127, 129
total trade receivables accounts (sales ledger control accounts) 127, 128
trade discount 26, 29, 45
trade payables 182
trade payables ledgers (purchases ledgers) 26, 27
trade payables turnover 181
trade receivables 70
trade receivables ledgers (sales ledgers) 26, 27

trade receivables turnover 180–1
trade unions 182
trading businesses 60, 61
trading section of income statements 61–2, 145
treasurers of clubs and societies 144
trial balances
   and income statements 62
   definition 19
   errors in 20–2
   errors not revealed by 22
   layout 20
   purpose and use 19
two column cash books 27

understandability of financial statements 79

value, residual 91

work in progress 162, 164
working capital 178, 180
written off debts 100, 101

Acknowledgements

Thanks to the following for permission to reproduce images:
Cover image: Sudarshan v/Getty Images